5th Workshop on Cognitive Modeling and Computational Linguistics

(CMCL 2014)

Held at ACL 2014

Baltimore, Maryland, USA
26 June 2014

ISBN: 978-1-63439-200-6

Printed from e-media with permission by:

Curran Associates, Inc.
57 Morehouse Lane
Red Hook, NY 12571

CURRAN ASSOCIATES INC. proceedings.com

Some format issues inherent in the e-media version may also appear in this print version.

Printed by Curran Associates, Inc. (2014)

Association for Computational Linguistics
209 N. Eighth Street
Stroudsburg, Pennsylvania 18360

Phone: 1-570-476-8006
Fax: 1-570-476-0860

acl@aclweb.org

Additional copies of this publication are available from:

Curran Associates, Inc.
57 Morehouse Lane
Red Hook, NY 12571 USA
Phone: 845-758-0400
Fax: 845-758-2634
Email: curran@proceedings.com
Web: www.proceedings.com

Introduction

The papers in these proceedings were presented at the 5th annual workshop on Cognitive Modeling and Computational Linguistics (CMCL), held in Baltimore, Maryland on June 26th, 2014. CMCL-2014 followed in the tradition of earlier CMCL meetings, providing a venue for research in mathematical and computational psycholinguistics. We solicited papers on a broad spectrum of topics which spanned the formal modeling of language representation, development, and processing, and were very pleased to receive 17 submissions this year. The program below includes 8 of these papers which were selected for final presentation at the workshop. We would like to thank all submitting authors for the quality and variety of the papers we received, and for helping to foster the growth of the field of computational psycholinguistics. We would also like to thank our program committee for providing expertise in the evaluation of submitted papers. Finally, our program this year includes invited talks by Dr. Naomi Feldman of the University of Maryland and Dr. Edward Gibson of the Massachusetts Institute of Technology. We extend our appreciation to these researchers for sharing their work with us.

Tim O'Donnell and Vera Demberg

Organizers:

Vera Demberg, Saarland University (Germany)
Tim O'Donnell, MIT (USA)

Program Committee:

Afra Alishahi, Tilburg University (The Netherlands)
Klinton Bicknell, Northwestern University (USA)
Alexander Clark, King's College London (UK)
Jennifer Culbertson, George Mason University (USA)
Afsaneh Fazly, University of Toronto (Canada)
Bob Frank, Yale (USA)
Stefan Frank, Radboud University Nijmegen (The Netherlands)
Stella Frank, University of Edinburgh (UK)
John T. Hale, Cornell University (USA)
Frank Keller, University of Edinburgh (UK)
Anna Korhonen, University of Cambridge (UK)
Shalom Lappin, King's College London (UK)
Richard L. Lewis, University of Michigan (USA)
Sebastian Padó, University of Stuttgart (Germany)
David Reitter, Penn State University (USA)
William Schuler, The Ohio State University (USA)
Nathaniel Smith, University of Edinburgh (UK)
Ed Stabler, UCLA (USA)
Mark Steedman, University of Edinburgh (UK)
Charles Yang, University of Pennsylvania (USA)
Jelle Zuidema, University of Amsterdam (The Netherlands)

Invited Speakers:

Edward Gibson, MIT (USA)
Naomi Feldman, University of Maryland (USA)

Table of Contents

Workshop Program

Thursday, June 26, 2014

8:55–9:00 Opening

9:00–10:00 Invited talk by Naomi Feldman

10:00–10:30 *Computationally Rational Saccadic Control: An Explanation of Spillover Effects Based on Sampling from Noisy Perception and Memory*
Michael Shvartsman, Richard Lewis and Satinder Singh

10:30–11:00 Coffee break

11:00–11:30 *Investigating the role of entropy in sentence processing*
Tal Linzen and Florian Jaeger

11:30–12:00 *Sentence Processing in a Vectorial Model of Working Memory*
William Schuler

12:00–12:30 *Evaluating Evaluation Metrics for Minimalist Parsing*
Thomas Graf and Bradley Marcinek

12:30–14:00 Lunch break

14:00–14:30 *Learning Verb Classes in an Incremental Model*
Libby Barak, Afsaneh Fazly and Suzanne Stevenson

14:30–15:00 *A Usage-Based Model of Early Grammatical Development*
Barend Beekhuizen, Rens Bod, Afsaneh Fazly, Suzanne Stevenson and Arie Verhagen

15:00–15:30 *A Model to Qualify the Linguistic Adaptation Phenomenon in Online Conversation Threads: Analyzing Priming Effect in Online Health Community*
Yafei Wang, David Reitter and John Yen

15:30–16:00 Coffee break

16:00–16:30 *Quantifying the role of discourse topicality in speakers' choices of referring expressions*
Naho Orita, Naomi Feldman, Jordan Boyd-Graber and Eliana Vornov

Thursday, June 26, 2014 (continued)

16:30–17:30 Invited talk by Ted Gibson

17:30–17:45 Closing Remarks

Computationally Rational Saccadic Control: An Explanation of Spillover Effects Based on Sampling from Noisy Perception and Memory

Michael Shvartsman
Department of Psychology
University of Michigan
mshvarts@umich.edu

Richard L. Lewis
Department of Psychology
University of Michigan
rickl@umich.edu

Satinder Singh
Computer Science & Eng.
University of Michigan
baveja@umich.edu

Abstract

Eye-movements in reading exhibit frequency spillover effects: fixation durations on a word are affected by the frequency of the previous word. We explore the idea that this effect may be an emergent property of a computationally rational eye-movement strategy that is navigating a tradeoff between processing immediate perceptual input, and continued processing of past input based on memory. We present an adaptive eye-movement control model with a minimal capacity for such processing, based on a composition of thresholded sequential samplers that integrate information from noisy perception and noisy memory. The model is applied to the *List Lexical Decision Task* and shown to yield frequency spillover—a robust property of human eye-movements in this task, even with parafoveal masking. We show that spillover in the model emerges in approximately optimal control policies that sometimes process memory rather than perception. We compare this model with one that is able to give priority to perception over memory, and show that the perception-priority policies in such a model do not perform as well in a range of plausible noise settings. We explain how the frequency spillover arises from a counter-intuitive but fundamental property of sequenced thresholded samplers.

1 Introduction and overview

Our interest is in understanding how eye-movements are controlled in service of linguistic tasks involving reading—more specifically, how saccadic decisions are conditioned on the moment-by-moment state of incremental perceptual and cognitive processing. The phenomena we are concerned with here are *spillover effects*, where fixation durations on a word are affected by linguistic properties of the prior word or words. The specific idea we explore is that spillover effects may be emergent properties of a computationally rational control strategy that is navigating a tradeoff between processing immediate perceptual input, and continued processing of past input based on a memory of recent stimuli.

The paper is organized as follows. We first review evidence that eye-movement control in reading is strategically adaptive, and describe our theoretical approach. We then review evidence from gaze-contingent eye-tracking paradigms—some existing and some new—that suggests that frequency spillover is not driven exclusively by parafoveal preview of upcoming words. We take this as evidence that frequency spillover may be driven in part by processing of words that continues after the eyes have moved away. We then extend an existing adaptive control model of eye-movements with a minimal capacity for such continued processing, by allowing it to process a memory of past input. The model is based on a simple composition of thresholded sequential samplers that integrate information from noisy perception and noisy memory. Threshold parameters define the control policy and their values determine how processing resources are allocated to perception and memory. We provide a computational rationality analysis of the model's policy space: First, we show that frequency spillover emerges in top-performing policies, where performance is evaluated on the same task and payoff given to human participants. Second, we show that a model capable of spillover does no worse than an otherwise identical model that can eliminate spillover by always attending to perception when it can, and that the spillover-capable policies in such a model do no worse than spillover-incapable ones across the speed-accuracy tradeoff curve, and in fact do better in some portions of the noise parameter space. Finally, we trace the origin of the effect to a counter-intuitive but fundamental property of the dynamics of sequenced thresholded samplers.

2 Adaptive control of eye-movements: Evidence and theoretical approach

A growing body of evidence suggests that eye-movements in reading are strategic adaptations that manifest at the level of individual fixations. For example, Rayner and Fischer (1996) showed

Proceedings of the 2014 ACL Workshop on Cognitive Modeling and Computational Linguistics, pages 1–9,
Baltimore, Maryland USA, June 26 2014. ©2014 Association for Computational Linguistics

that when participants are searching for a particular word in a text rather than reading for full comprehension, saccade durations are shortened and the magnitude of frequency effects is reduced. Wotschack (2009) showed that readers assigned the task of proofreading read more slowly and performed more second-pass reading with fewer skips than in a control reading-for-comprehension task.

People also adapt reading behavior to within-task manipulations of difficulty and payoff. Wotschack (2009) showed that people change their reading behavior in response to manipulations of the difficulty of comprehension questions. Lewis et al. (2013) showed that people adapt their eye movements in response to changes in quantitative task payoffs. Payoffs emphasizing speed at the expense of accuracy result in shorter fixation durations and lower accuracies.

We seek to develop a model that can explain such variation in eye-movement behavior as a rational adaptation to the task (including utility) and the internal oculomotor and cognitive architecture (Lewis et al., 2013). Such a model would permit a *computational rationality* analysis (Lewis et al., to appear) because the problem of rational behavior is defined in part by the bounded mechanisms of the posited computational architecture.

We constrain our architectural assumptions by building on existing theories of oculomotor architecture, such as E-Z Reader (Reichle et al., 2009). But we enrich these architectures with explicit assumptions about the policy space of saccadic control, and with assumptions about the processing of noisy perception and memory. This enriched architecture is then embedded in a minimal cognitive system that is capable of performing a complete experimental task. The complete model affords computational rationality analyses because it can be used to derive the implications of saccadic control policies for task performance.

3 The nature of spillover effects

Our aim in this section is to establish a link between spillover and the continued processing of past input based on memory. Consider a pair of words in sequence: word$_{n-1}$ and word$_n$. There are three natural explanations for how the frequency of word$_{n-1}$ could affect the duration of fixations on word$_n$. (1) During fixation of word$_n$, perceptual information from word$_{n-1}$ is available in the parafovea and continues to be processed.

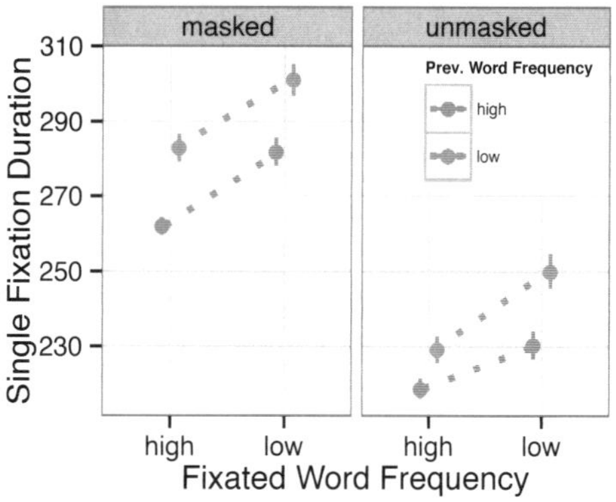

Figure 1: *Frequency spillover in the List Lexical Decision Task.* Single fixation durations (fixations when the word was fixated only once) on words as a function of the fixated and previous word's frequency. Frequencies are binned by a median split; error bars are bootstrapped standard errors.

We call this the *parafoveal review* explanation. (2) During fixation on word$_{n-1}$, perceptual information from word$_n$ is available in the parafovea; the frequency of word$_{n-1}$ affects the degree to which this information is processed, and this in turns affects the subsequent fixation duration on word$_n$. We call this the *parafoveal preview* explanation. (3) During fixation of word$_n$, processing of word$_{n-1}$ continues based on some memory of the perception of word$_{n-1}$, and this processing is affected by the frequency of word$_{n-1}$. We call this the *memory* explanation.

It is unlikely that spillover is driven by parafoveal review because the effective visual field in reading does not extend to the left of the current word (Rayner et al., 1980).

The standard paradigm for investigating the relationship between spillover effects and parafoveal preview is some form of parafoveal masking (Rayner, 1975): a nonveridical preview of word$_n$ is shown until the eye crosses an invisible boundary just before word$_n$, at which point word$_n$ is shown. When participants are not informed of the manipulation or do not notice it, they do not exhibit frequency spillover (Henderson and Ferreira, 1990; Kennison and Clifton, 1995; White et al., 2005). However, when participants are aware of preview being unavailable or not veridical, the spillover frequency effect remains (White et al., 2005; Schroyens et al., 1999). These results suggest that parafoveal preview (or review) cannot be the only explanation of spillover and therefore the

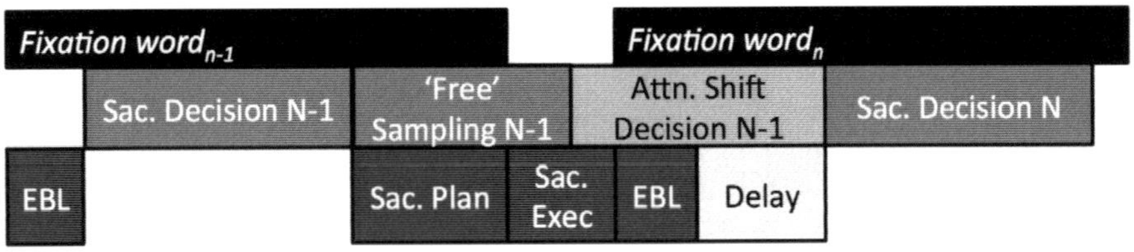

Figure 2: *Example dynamics of a decision to saccade from word$_{n-1}$ to word$_n$.* The memory-driven attention shift decision can delay the start of perceptual sampling on the next word, potentially creating spillover. A detailed description of the dynamics depicted in this figure is in §4.

memory explanation warrants consideration. We now summarize unpublished data consistent with these findings in a simple linguistic task that we also use to test the new model reported below.

Spillover in the List Lexical Decision Task (LLDT). We use the List Lexical Decision Task (LLDT) (Lewis et al., 2013), an extension of a task introduced by Meyer and Schvaneveldt (1971). In the LLDT participants must determine whether a list of six strings contains all words, or contains a single nonword. All strings are four characters in length and separated by six character spaces. The task was designed to require sequential eye-movements and contact with the mental lexicon (but not higher-level linguistic processing), to minimize parafoveal processing (via the wide spacing), and to yield a high proportion of single-fixation durations (via short strings).

Two versions of the task were performed by separate participant groups. In the masked condition, we used a gaze-contingent moving window paradigm wherein all strings but the fixated string were replaced with hashmarks (####). In the unmasked condition, all six strings remained visible.

Figure 1 shows the effects of word frequency on single fixation durations. The main result of current interest is that frequency spillover is evident in both conditions, despite the wide spacing in the unmasked condition, and the complete denial of parafoveal preview in the masked condition.

The work reviewed above and our new data are consistent with an account of spillover in which both parafoveal preview (if available) and memory-based processing are operative. Our concern here is with the latter: understanding how a noisy memory of recently seen stimuli might be incorporated into an adaptive oculomotor architecture, and exploring whether rational exploitation of that memory might lead to spillover.

4 A model of saccadic control with noisy memory for recent perception

Our new model extends the one presented in Lewis et al. (2013) to include a noisy memory that buffers perceptual input. We develop it in the context of the LLDT, but its essential elements are not tied to this task. It is most easily understood by first considering the dynamics of a single decision to saccade from one word to the next, as presented in Figure 2. After describing these dynamics we summarize the model's key assumptions and associated mathematical specification.

The dynamics of a decision to saccade from word$_{n-1}$ to word$_n$. The eye first fixates word$_{n-1}$. Some time passes before information from the retina becomes available for perceptual processing (the eye-brain lag, EBL in Figure 2). A sequence of noisy perceptual samples then arrive and are integrated via an incremental and noisy Bayesian update of a probability distribution over lexical hypotheses in a manner described below. The perceptual samples are also buffered by storing them in a memory that contains samples from only one word. When the probability of one of the hypotheses reaches the *saccade threshold*, saccade planning is initiated. Perceptual sampling (marked as *free sampling* in Figure 2 because its length is not under adaptive control) continues in parallel with saccade planning until the fixation ends, and then for another EBL amount longer (these are samples received at the retina during the fixation and only now arriving at the lexical processor).

The model then switches to sampling from its memory, continuing to update the distribution over lexical hypotheses until one of the hypotheses reaches an *attention shift threshold*. If this threshold had already been reached during the earlier perceptual sampling stages, attention shifts instantly. Otherwise attention remains on word$_{n-1}$ even if the eye has saccaded to word$_n$, and the eye-brain lag on word$_n$ is completed. Perceptual samples from word$_n$ will not be processed until attention is shifted away from the memory-based processing of word$_{n-1}$. Thus the memory processing on word$_{n-1}$ may delay processing of perceptual samples from word$_n$; perceptual samples arriving during this time are buffered in the memory. In this way the posterior update is a limited computational resource and its relative allocation to perception or memory is determined by the saccade and attention shift thresholds. To the extent that the time to reach the attention shift threshold is sensitive to the frequency of word$_{n-1}$, the model may exhibit a spillover frequency effect.

Lexical processing as rise-to-threshold decisionmaking. The decisions to plan a saccade, shift attention, and make a motor response are realized as Multi-hypothesis Sequential Probability Ratio Tests (Baum and Veeravalli, 1994; Dragalin et al., 2000). At each timestep, the model performs a Bayes update based on a noisy sample drawn from perception or memory, with the posterior at each timestep becoming the prior for the next timestep. Our choice of word representation follows Norris (2006) in representing a letter as a unit-basis vector encoding and a word as a concatenation of such vectors.

To generate a perceptual sample, mean-zero Gaussian *perception noise* with standard deviation (SD) σ_p is added to each component of the word representation vector. Each perceptual sample is also stored in a memory buffer, and memory samples are generated by uniformly drawing a stored sample from memory (with replacement), and adding an additional mean-zero Gaussian *memory noise* with SD σ_m to each position. Before each Bayesian update, whether using a sample from perception or memory, mean-zero Gaussian *update noise* with SD σ_u is added to each component of the word representation vector. Thus a Bayes update from a perceptual sample includes two noise terms, while a Bayes update from a memory sample includes three noise terms. All noises are drawn independently. The three SD's, σ_p, σ_m and σ_u, are free parameters in the model, and we explore their implications below.

The model uses the update specified in the appendix in Lewis et al. (2013) except for the noise generation specified above and the consequent change in the likelihood computation. The lexical hypotheses are updated as follows:

$$Pr_{new}(S^k|s^k, \mathcal{T}) = \frac{Pr(s^k|S^k, \mathcal{T})Pr_{old}(S^k, \mathcal{T})}{\sum_S Pr(s^k|S^k, \mathcal{T})Pr_{old}(S^k, \mathcal{T})} \quad (1)$$

where s^k is a sample generated as above from the letterstring (word or nonword) in the current position k, S^k is the hypothesis that the string at position k is S, and $\mathcal{T}$ is a multinomial distribution reflecting the current belief of (a) whether this is an all-words trial and (b) otherwise, where the nonword is located. The eye movement planning and attention shift decisions are conditioned on the distribution of probabilities $Pr(S^k)$ for all strings in the current position. When the maximum of these probabilities crosses a saccade planning threshold θ_s, saccade planning begins. When the maximum crosses the attention shift threshold θ_a, attention shifts to the next word[1]. Each sample takes 10ms, a fixed discretization parameter.

The likelihood of drawing perceptual or memory sample s for a string S is computed from the unit-basis word representation as follows:

$$Pr(s|S) = \prod_i f(s_i; \mu_i, \sigma) \quad (2)$$

where i indexes the unit-basis vector representation of sample s and some true letterstring S (and so μ_i is either 0 or 1), σ is the sampling noise (dependent on whether the samples are memory or perceptual samples as specified below), and $f(x; \mu, \sigma)$ is the probability density function of the normal distribution with mean μ and standard deviation σ.

We simplify the likelihood computation for memory samples by treating the perception and memory samples as independent. For present purposes this assumption may be treated as a bound on the architecture. The σ in Equation 2 is $\sqrt{(\sigma_p^2 + \sigma_u^2)}$ for perceptual samples and $\sqrt{(\sigma_p^2 + \sigma_m^2 + \sigma_u^2)}$ for memory samples. At each sample the string-level probabilities in each position are aggregated to the multinomial trial-level decision variable $\mathcal{T}$ as described above. Given $\mathcal{T}$ the model computes the probability of a word trial $Pr(\mathcal{W})$ or nonword trial $Pr(\mathcal{N}) = 1 - Pr(\mathcal{W})$. When either of these probabilities exceeds the motor response threshold θ_r, motor response planning commences.

[1] Because there is a fixed set of memory samples available, the attention shift decision is not guaranteed to converge, unlike the saccade threshold. It nearly always converges, but we use a 30-sample deadline to prevent infinite sequences.

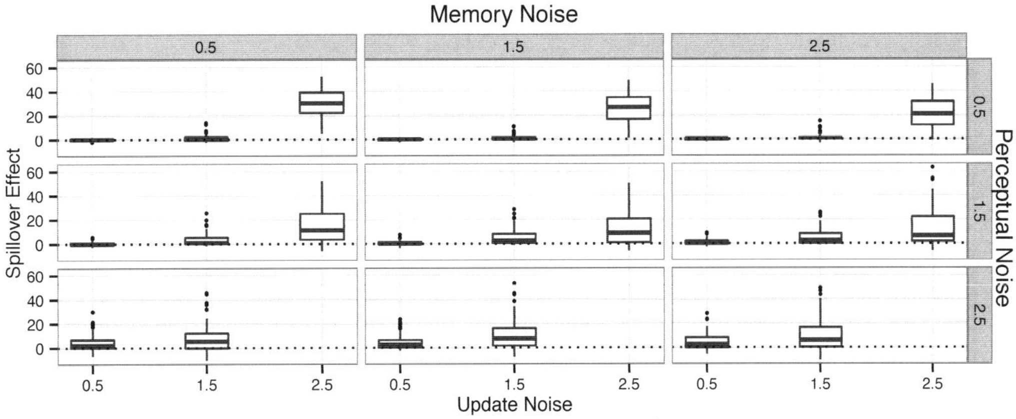

Figure 3: *Spillover effects generated by the top 5% of policies across different settings of memory, perception, and update noise.* On each distinct machine defined by a combination of noise settings, policies (settings of $\theta_s, \theta_m, \theta_r$) were evaluated by the same task payoff given to human participants in the experiment described in §3. Boxplots show spillover effects of the top-performing 5% of policies. Spillover effects are the difference in mean single fixation durations on word_n when word_{n-1} is low frequency and when word_{n-1} is high frequency (low/high determined by median split). The highest noise settings in the bottom row are not shown because performance was near-chance even for the best policies.

The prior probability of an all-words trial is 0.5, so the prior probability of a word in each position k is $1 - \frac{0.5}{6}$. Therefore, we set the prior probabilities of words in each position to corpus frequency counts (Kučera and Francis, 1967), normalized to sum to this value, $1 - \frac{0.5}{6}$. Nonword probabilities are uniformly distributed over the remainder, $\frac{0.5}{6}$.

Oculomotor and Manual Architecture. The remainder of the architectural parameters are stage durations that are simulated as gamma deviates with means based on previous work or independently estimated from data. The key parameters for present purposes are the 50ms mean eye-brain lag and 125ms saccade planning time, following Reichle et al. (2009), and the 40ms mean saccade execution time, based on estimates from our own human participants. The standard deviation of each distribution is 0.3 times the mean. We transform the means and standard deviations into scale and shape parameters for a Gamma distribution and then draw duration values from these Gammas independently for every word and trial.

5 A computational rationality analysis

We explore whether spillover effects might be a signature of computationally rational behavior in two ways. First, we evaluate a space of policies (parameterized by $\theta_s, \theta_m, \theta_r$) against the task payoff given to our human participants, and show that top-performing policies yield frequency spillover consistent with human data, and poor-performing policies do not. Second, we extend the model's policy space to allow it to prioritize perception over memory samples when both are available (eliminating spillover in those policies), and show that the spillover portions of the policy space perform better than non-spillover ones under any imposed speed-accuracy tradeoff in plausible noise settings, and never perform worse.

In computational rationality analyses, we distinguish between policy parameters, fixed architecture parameters, and free architecture parameters. Policy parameters are determined by selecting those policies that maximize a given task payoff, given the hypothesized architectural bounds. Fixed architecture parameters are based on previous empirical or theoretical work. Free architecture parameters can be fit to data or explored to show the range of predictions with which the model is compatible. We focus here on the latter, showing not only that the model is compatible with human data, but that it is incompatible with results significantly different from the human data.

Our first evaluation of the model asks the question of whether we see spillover effects emerging in approximately optimal policies under our assumptions about mechanism and task. We evaluated our model in the LLDT, under the balanced payoff presented in Lewis et al. (2013), the same

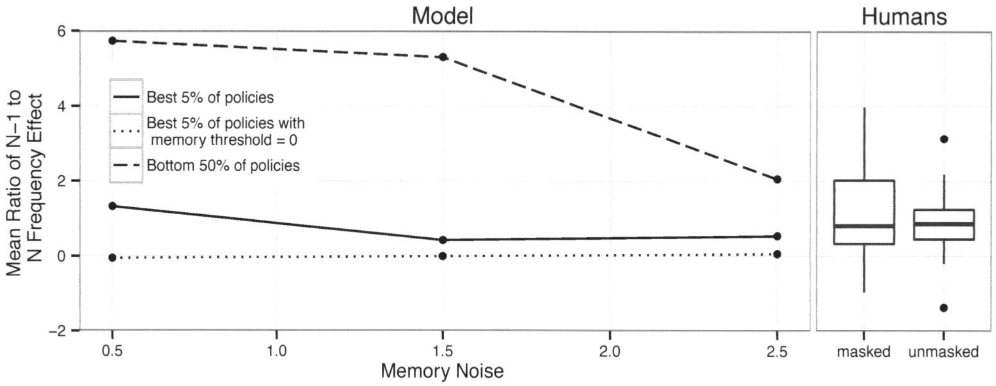

Figure 4: *Normalized spillover effect in model (vs. memory noise) and human participants.* We define normalized spillover as the ratio of the spillover (word_{n-1}) frequency effect size to the foveal (word_n) frequency effect size; this normalizes against scale differences between high and low noise architectures. *Left*: Mean normalized spillover effect at different memory noises for best performing 5% of policies with and without memory sampling, and worst 50% performing policies. *Right*: Mean human spillover effect sizes in masked and unmasked versions of LLDT.

payoff given to our participants in the unpublished masking experiment described above. We explored a discretized policy space as follows: we let θ_s range between 0.199 and 0.999 in steps of 0.05; θ_m between 0.19999 and 0.99999 in steps of 0.05, and also include $\theta_m = 0$ which prevents memory sampling; and θ_r between 0.599 and 0.999 in steps of 0.1. We explored all 1530 permutations.

Figure 3 shows the distribution of spillover effect sizes in the top 5% of policies (evaluated by task payoff, not fit to human data), for a range of noise parameter settings (at higher noise settings, even the best policies are close to chance performance). The top 5% of policies average 7.78 points per trial across the noise and policy range, and the bottom 50% average 1.32 points. The figure shows that top-performing policies show little to no spillover when update noise is low, positive but small spillover effects when update noise is moderate, and sizable positive spillover effects when update noise is relatively high. These results are consistent with spillover as a rational adaptation to belief update noise.

Figure 4 (left panel) shows normalized spillover effects (the ratio of the word_{n-1} frequency effect to the word_n frequency effect) for the best policies, the bottom 50% of policies, and the best policies constrained with a memory threshold of zero ($\theta_m = 0$). When $\theta_m = 0$, the spillover effect is zero as expected. The top performing policies in the unconstrained space generate nonzero spillover effects that are consistent with the human data, but the poor performing policies do not (Figure 4, right panel). We know that the top performing policies exploit memory because they do yield nonzero spillover effects, and the values of θ_m are nonzero for these policies.

Our second evaluation asks whether a model that is constrained to always give priority to processing perceptual samples over memory samples will perform better than the present model, which has the flexibility to give priority to memory over perception. To explore this, we added a single binary policy parameter, the *perceptual priority* bit. If this bit is set, then the model has the choice between memory sampling from word_{n-1} and perceptual sampling from word_n, it always chooses the latter. Such an option is not available in the previous model—there is no setting of the saccade and memory thresholds that will always use memory samples when only they are available, but also never choose to use memory samples when perceptual samples can be used. With the perceptual priority bit set, the model is capable of exploiting the least noisy samples available to it, but is incapable of exhibiting spillover effects.

Figure 5 shows speed-accuracy tradeoffs for the model, with the perceptual-priority bit not set (spillover-capable) and set (spillover-incapable), in three representative noise settings. Individual points are policies and the lines mark the best accuracy available at a particular reaction time for the two classes of policies; i.e. these lines represent the best speed-accuracy tradeoff possible for

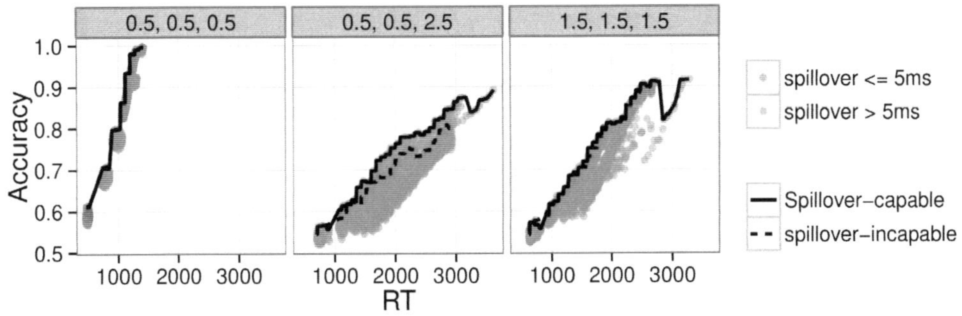

Figure 5: *Speed-accuracy tradeoff curves for some representative noise settings.* Each individual point corresponds to one policy (i.e. setting of the three decision thresholds). Plotted are mean trial RT and accuracy (computed from 5000 simulated trials), color-coded by whether the policies yielded spillover frequency effects. Lines mark the best speed-accuracy tradeoff available to spillover-capable and incapable policies. Each plot is labeled at the top with the noise setting *(perceptual, memory, update)*.

both spillover-capable and -incapable policies. In the left plot of the figure, noise is low enough overall such that responses are very fast and spillover-capable policies do no worse and no better than spillover-incapable policies. In the middle plot, update noise is higher, and the optimal speed-accuracy tradeoff is better for the model that can yield spillover, consistent with the exploitation of memory sampling to mitigate update noise. In the right plot, perception and memory noise are high enough that it is not useful to sample from memory at the expense of perception. All the noise settings we explored (see Figure 3 for the range) yield one of these three patterns, or the uninteresting case of near-chance performance. In no setting does the spillover-capable model perform worse than the spillover-incapable one. The noise settings cover a range from implausibly-high accuracy to chance performance, and so we conclude that spillover-capable policies dominate, in that they do no worse, and occasionally do better, than those constrained to give priority to perception over memory.

6 Why spillover arises from sequenced thresholded samplers

We have demonstrated through simulations that the model yields frequency spillover through a composed sequence of perception and memory sampling. We have not yet addressed the question of how or why this happens. Indeed, it is initially somewhat puzzling that an effect of priors (set by lexical frequency) would persist after the initial perceptual sampling threshold θ_p is passed, because this fixed threshold must be exceeded no matter the starting prior.

The crucial insight is that it is not always the case that the true word hypothesis reaches the threshold first; i.e., the decision to initiate saccade planning may be based on (partial) recognition of a different word than the true word. In such cases, at the start of memory sampling, the hypothesis for the true word is farther from the memory threshold θ_m than if the true word had been (partially) recognized. Incorrect decisions are more likely for low frequency words, so in expectation the memory-driven attention shift mechanism will start farther from its threshold for low-frequency words, and therefore take longer to reach threshold, delaying the following word more.

We constructed a minimal two-sampler example to clearly illustrate this phenomenon. The leftmost panel of Figure 6 illustrates the dynamics of such a trial. In this panel, the threshold is crossed for the incorrect hypothesis (green line) in the first sampler, triggering the start of the second sampler. The second sampler recovers from the mistake, allowing the correct (red) hypothesis to cross the threshold, but at the cost of additional time. The middle panel shows that incorrect (and thus eligible for recovery) trials are more frequent for low priors. The rightmost panel shows that the finishing time of the second sampler is proportional to the prior probability of the correct hypothesis for the first sampler. It is also inversely proportional to accuracy (middle plot), consistent with inaccurate trials driving the relationship between the first sampler prior and second sampler finishing times.

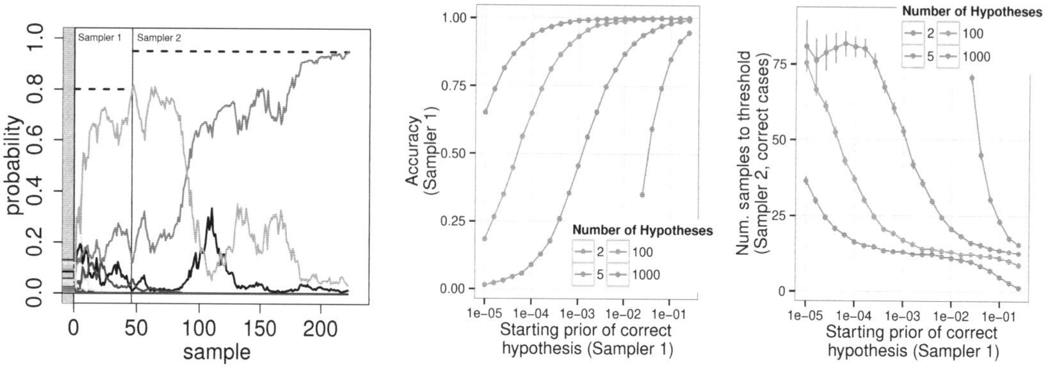

Figure 6: *A simple example illustrating how the prior for a thresholded sampler affects its final posterior, and therefore the prior for a subsequent coupled sampler, despite the fixed threshold. Left*: An example 'recovery' trial for 500 hypotheses (words). *Middle*: Accuracy for the first sampler as a function of the prior of the true hypothesis. *Right*: Second sampler finishing times as a function of to the true-hypothesis prior in the first sampler.

7 Discussion and Conclusion

We briefly highlight the key properties of the model that yield our result and how they may generalize beyond our particular implementation.

Post-perceptual processing. Although we adopted a second MSPRT sampler, spillover may arise from other processes with access to the posterior of the perceptual sampling, such that it can recover from perceptually misidentified words. In the present model we investigated the possibility that post-perceptual memory-based processing could be partially motivated by mitigating noise in the update process itself. But it is almost certainly the case that post-perceptual processing is required in the course of reading for independent reasons, and such processing could also yield spillover frequency effects in a way that the memory sampling process does. (A challenge for such an alternate process is that spillover effects persist in the LLDT in the absence of required higher level syntactic or semantic processing).

A tradeoff between processing perception and memory. The serial queuing model is a simple realization (inspired by EZ-Reader (Reichle et al., 1998)) of a limited resource that can be allocated to perceptual and memory processing, but an alternative parallel attention machine might recover the results, as long as it suffers from the same tradeoff that processing the previous word from memory will slow down processing of the fixated word.

Direct oculomotor control. In the present model saccade planning is triggered directly by the perceptual evidence accumulation process, and as such is not obviously compatible with autonomous saccade generation models like SWIFT (Engbert et al., 2005). It may be possible to layer SWIFT's time-delayed foveal inhibition over a sequential sampling process, but we note that spillover effects were part of the empirical motivation for such delayed control.

The present model and results open several avenues for future work. These include the interactions of memory-based or post-perceptual processing with models of saccade planning that include saccade targeting, re-targeting, and cancellation, as well as buttonpress behavior (e.g. in the self-paced moving window paradigm). The role that parafoveal preview plays in spillover effects can also be explored, including how the model (and thus human participants) might navigate the tradeoff between using parafoveal preview information (noisy due to eccentricity) and using memory of past input in the service of a reading task. Finally, it is possible to explore the spillover explanation in an architecture capable of higher-level sentence processing in service of different reading task goals.

Acknowledgments

This material is based upon work supported by the National Science Foundation under Grant BCS-1152819 to RL and SB. We thank MindModeling@Home for invaluable computational resources.

References

C.W. Baum and V.V. Veeravalli. 1994. A sequential procedure for multihypothesis testing. *IEEE Transactions on Information Theory*, 40(6):1994–2007.

Vladimir P Dragalin, Alexander G Tartakovsky, Venugopal V Veeravalli, and Senior Member. 2000. Multihypothesis Sequential Probability Ratio Tests Part II : Accurate Asymptotic Expansions for the Expected Sample Size. *IEEE Transactions on Information Theory*, 46(4):1366–1383.

Ralf Engbert, Antje Nuthmann, Eike M. Richter, and Reinhold Kliegl. 2005. SWIFT: a dynamical model of saccade generation during reading. *Psychological review*, 112(4):777–813, October.

John M. Henderson and Fernanda Ferreira. 1990. Effects of foveal processing difficulty on the perceptual span in reading: Implications for attention and eye movement control. *Journal of Experimental Psychology: Learning, Memory, and Cognition*, 16(3):417–429.

Sheila M. Kennison and Charles Clifton. 1995. Determinants of parafoveal preview benefit in high and low working memory capacity readers: implications for eye movement control. *Journal of experimental psychology. Learning, memory, and cognition*, 21(1):68–81, January.

Henry Kučera and W. Nelson Francis. 1967. *Computational analysis of present-day American English*. Brown University Press, Providence, RI.

Richard L. Lewis, Michael Shvartsman, and Satinder Singh. 2013. The Adaptive Nature of Eye Movements in Linguistic Tasks: How Payoff and Architecture Shape Speed-Accuracy Trade-Offs. *Topics in cognitive science*, pages 1–30, June.

Richard L. Lewis, Andrew Howes, and Satinder Singh. to appear. Computational rationality: Linking mechanism and behavior through utility maximization. *Topics in Cognitive Science*.

David E. Meyer and Roger Schvaneveldt. 1971. Facilitation in recognizing pairs of words: Evidence of a dependence between retrieval operations. *Journal of Experimental Psychology*, 90:22–34.

Dennis Norris. 2006. The Bayesian reader: explaining word recognition as an optimal Bayesian decision process. *Psychological review*, 113(2):327–357, April.

Keith Rayner and Martin H. Fischer. 1996. Mindless reading revisited: eye movements during reading and scanning are different. *Perception & psychophysics*, 58(5):734–47, July.

Keith Rayner, Arnold D. Well, and Alexander Pollatsek. 1980. Asymmetry of the effective visual field in reading. *Perception & psychophysics*, 27(6):537–44, June.

Keith Rayner. 1975. The perceptual span and peripheral cues in reading. *Cognitive Psychology*, 7(1):65–81, January.

E D Reichle, a Pollatsek, D L Fisher, and K Rayner. 1998. Toward a model of eye movement control in reading. *Psychological review*, 105(1):125–57, January.

Erik D. Reichle, Tessa Warren, and Kerry McConnell. 2009. Using E-Z Reader to model the effects of higher level language processing on eye movements during reading. *Psychonomic bulletin & review*, 16(1):1–21, February.

Walter Schroyens, Françoise Vitu, Marc Brysbaert, and Géry D'Ydewalle. 1999. Eye movement control during reading: foveal load and parafoveal processing. *The Quarterly journal of experimental psychology*, 52(4):1021–46, November.

Sarah J. White, Keith Rayner, and Simon P. Liversedge. 2005. Eye movements and the modulation of parafoveal processing by foveal processing difficulty: A reexamination. *Psychonomic bulletin & review*, 12(5):891–6, October.

Christiane Wotschack. 2009. *Eye Movements in Reading Strategies*. Ph.D. thesis.

Investigating the role of entropy in sentence processing

Tal Linzen
Department of Linguistics
New York University
linzen@nyu.edu

T. Florian Jaeger
Brain and Cognitive Sciences
University of Rochester
fjaeger@bcs.rochester.edu

Abstract

We outline four ways in which uncertainty might affect comprehension difficulty in human sentence processing. These four hypotheses motivate a self-paced reading experiment, in which we used verb subcategorization distributions to manipulate the uncertainty over the next step in the syntactic derivation (single step entropy) and the surprisal of the verb's complement. We additionally estimate word-by-word surprisal and total entropy over parses of the sentence using a probabilistic context-free grammar (PCFG). Surprisal and total entropy, but not single step entropy, were significant predictors of reading times in different parts of the sentence. This suggests that a complete model of sentence processing should incorporate both entropy and surprisal.

1 Introduction

Predictable linguistic elements are processed faster than unpredictable ones. Specifically, processing load on an element A in context C is linearly correlated with its surprisal, $-\log_2 P(A|C)$ (Smith and Levy, 2013). This suggests that readers maintain expectations as to the upcoming elements: likely elements are accessed or constructed in advance of being read. While there is substantial amount of work on the effect of predictability on processing difficulty, the role (if any) of the distribution over expectations is less well understood.

Surprisal predicts that the distribution over competing predicted elements should not affect reading times: if the conditional probability of a word A is $P(A|C)$, reading times on the word will be proportional to $-\log_2 P(A|C)$, regardless of whether the remaining probability mass is distributed among two or a hundred options.

The **entropy reduction hypothesis** (Hale, 2003; Hale, 2006), on the other hand, accords a central role to the distribution over predicted parses. According to this hypothesis, an incoming element is costly to process when it entails a change from a state of high uncertainty (e.g., multiple equiprobable parses) to a state of low uncertainty (e.g., one where a single parse is much more likely than the others). Uncertainty is quantified as the entropy of the distribution over complete parses of the sentence; that is, if A^i is the set of all possible parses of the sentence after word w_i, then the uncertainty following w_i is given by

$$H_{w_i} = -\sum_{a \in A^i} P(a) \log_2 P(a) \quad (1)$$

Processing load in this hypothesis is proportional to the entropy reduction caused by w_n:[1]

$$\text{ER}(w_n) = \max\{H_{w_{n-1}} - H_{w_n}, 0\} \quad (2)$$

A third hypothesis, which we term the **competition hypothesis**, predicts that higher competition among potential outcomes should result in increased processing load at the point at which the competing parses are still valid (McRae et al., 1998; Tabor and Tanenhaus, 1999). This contrasts with the entropy reduction hypothesis, according to which processing cost arises when competition is *resolved*. Intuitively, the two hypotheses make inversely correlated predictions: on average, there will be less competition following words that reduce entropy. A recent study found that reading times on w_i correlated positively with entropy following w_i, providing support for this hypothesis (Roark et al., 2009).

The fourth hypothesis we consider, which we term the **commitment hypothesis**, is derived from

[1] No processing load is predicted for words that increase uncertainty.

Proceedings of the 2014 ACL Workshop on Cognitive Modeling and Computational Linguistics, pages 10–18,
Baltimore, Maryland USA, June 26 2014.

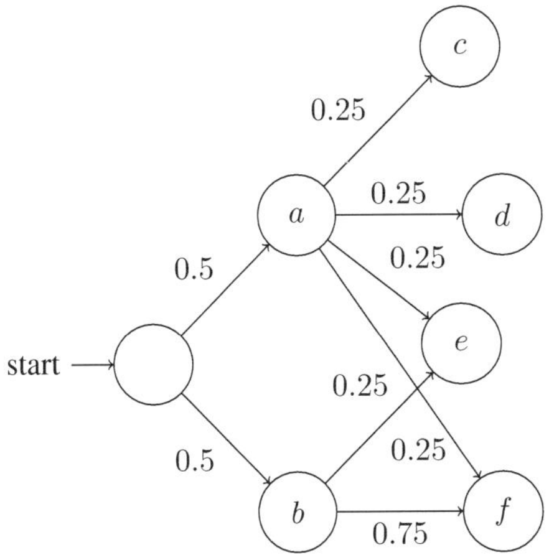

Figure 1: Example language. Output strings are indicated inside the nodes, and transition probabilities are indicated on the edges. For example, the probability of the sentence bf is 0.5×0.75.

the event-related potential (ERP) literature on contextual constraint. Studies in this tradition have compared the responses to a low-predictability word across two types of context: high-constraint contexts, in which there is a strong expectation for a (different) word, and low-constraint ones, which are not strongly predictive of any individual word. There is increasing evidence for an ERP component that responds to violations of a strong prediction (Federmeier, 2007; Van Petten and Luka, 2012). This component can be interpreted as reflecting disproportional commitment to high probability predictions at the expense of lower probability ones, a more extreme version of the proposal that low-probability parses are pruned in the presence of a high-probability parse (Jurafsky, 1996). Surprisal is therefore expected to have a larger effect in high constraint contexts, in which entropy was low before the word being read. Commitment to a high probability prediction may also result in increased processing load at the point at which the commitment is made.

We illustrate these four hypotheses using the simple language sketched in Figure 1. Consider the predictions made by the four hypotheses for the sentences ae and be. Surprisal predicts no difference in reading times between these sentences, since the conditional probabilities of the words in the two sentences are identical (0.5 and 0.25 respectively).

The competition hypothesis predicts increased reading times on the first word in ae compared to be, because the entropy following a is higher than the entropy following b (2 bits compared to 0.71). Since all sentences in the language are two word long, entropy goes down to 0 after the second word in both sentences. This hypothesis therefore does not predict a reading time difference on the second word e.

Moving on to the entropy reduction hypothesis, five of the six possible sentences in the language have probability 0.5×0.25, and the sixth one (bf) has probability 0.5×0.75. The full entropy of the grammar is therefore 2.4 bits. The first word reduces entropy in both ae and be (to 2 and 0.71 bits respectively), but entropy reduction is higher when the first word is b. The entropy reduction hypothesis therefore predicts longer reading times on the first word in be than in ae. Conversely, since entropy goes down to 0 in both cases, but from 2 bits in ae compared to 0.71 bits in be, this hypothesis predicts longer reading times on e in ae than in be.

Finally, the commitment hypothesis predicts that after b the reader will become committed to the prediction that the second word will be f. This will lead to longer reading times on e in be than in ae, despite the fact that its conditional probability is identical in both cases. If commitment to a prediction entails additional work, this hypothesis predicts longer reading times on the first word when it is b.

This paper presents an reading time study that aims to test these hypotheses. Empirical tests of computational theories of sentence processing have employed either reading time corpora (Demberg and Keller, 2008) or controlled experimental materials (Yun et al., 2010). The current paper adopts the latter approach, trading off a decrease in lexical and syntactic heterogeneity for increased control. This paper is divided into two parts. Section 2 describes a reading time experiment, which tested the predictions of the surprisal, competition and commitment hypotheses, as applied to the entropy over the next single step in the syntactic derivation.[2] We then calculate the total entropy (up to an unbounded number of derivation steps) at each word using a PCFG; Section 3 describes how this grammar was constructed, overviews the predictions that it yielded in light of the four hypotheses, and evaluates these predictions on the results of the reading time experiment.

[2]We do not test the predictions of the entropy reduction hypothesis in this part of the paper, since that theory explicitly only applies to total rather than single-step entropy.

2 Reading time experiment

2.1 Design

To keep syntactic structure constant while manipulating surprisal and entropy over the next derivation step, we took advantage of the fact that verbs vary in the probability distribution of their syntactic complements (subcategorization frames). Several studies have demonstrated that readers are sensitive to subcategorization probabilities (Trueswell et al., 1993; Garnsey et al., 1997).

The structure of the experimental materials is shown in Table 1. In a 2x2x2 factorial design, we crossed the surprisal of a sentential complement (SC) given the verb, the entropy of the verb's subcategorization distribution, and the presence or absence of the complementizer *that*. When the complementizer is absent, the region *the island* is ambiguous between a direct object and an embedded subject.

Surprisal theory predicts an effect of SC surprisal on the disambiguating region in ambiguous sentences (sentences without *that*), as obtained in previous studies (Garnsey et al., 1997), and an effect of SC surprisal on the complementizer *that* in unambiguous sentences. Reading times should not differ at the verb: in the minimal context we used (*the men*), the surprisal of the verb should be closely approximated by its lexical frequency, which was matched across conditions.

The competition hypothesis predicts a positive main effect of subcategorization frame entropy (subcategorization frame entropy) at the verb: higher uncertainty over the syntactic category of the complement should result in slower reading times.

The commitment hypothesis predicts that the effect of surprisal in the disambiguating region should be amplified when subcategorization frame entropy is low, since the readers will have committed to the competing high probability frame. If the commitment step in itself incurs a processing cost, there should be a negative main effect of subcategorization frame entropy at the verb.

This experimental design varies the entropy over the single next derivation step: it assumes that the parser only predicts the identity of the subcategorization frame, but not its internal structure. Since the predictions of the entropy reduction hypothesis crucially depend on predicting the internal structure as well, we defer the discussion of that hypothesis until Section 3.

The men	discovered	(that)	the island
mat. subj.	*verb*	*that*	*emb. subj.*

had been invaded	by the enemy.
emb. verb complex	*rest*

Table 1: Structure of experimental materials (mat. = matrix, emb. = embedded, subj. = subject).

2.2 Methods

2.2.1 Participants

128 participants were recruited through Amazon Mechanical Turk and were paid \$1.75 for their participation.

2.2.2 Materials

32 verbs were selected from the Gahl et al. (2004) subcategorization frequency database, in 4 conditions: high vs. low SC surprisal and high vs. low subcategorization frame entropy (see Table 2). Verbs were matched across conditions for length in characters and for frequency in SUBTLEX-US corpus (Brysbaert and New, 2009). A sentence was created for each verb, following the structure in Table 1. Each sentence had two versions: one with the complementizer *that* after the verb and one without it. The matrix subjects were minimally informative two-word NPs (e.g. *the men*). Following the complementizer (or the verb, if the complementizer was omitted) was a definite NP (*the island*), which was always a plausible direct object of the matrix verb.

The embedded verb complex region consisted of three words: two auxiliary verbs (*had been*) or an auxiliary verb and negation (*would not*), followed by a past participle form (*invaded*). Each of the function words appeared the same number of times in each condition. The embedded verb complex was followed by three more words. The nouns and verbs in the embedded clause were matched for frequency and length across conditions.

In addition to the target sentences, the experiment contained 64 filler sentences, with various complex syntactic structures.

2.2.3 Procedure

The sentences were presented word by word in a self-paced moving window paradigm. The participants were presented with a Y/N comprehension question after each trial. The participants did not

	NP	Inf	PP	SC	SC s.	SFE
forget	0.55	0.14	0.2	0.09	3.46	1.7
hear	0.72	0	0.17	0.11	3.22	1.12
claim	0.36	0.12	0	0.45	1.15	1.71
sense	0.61	0	0.02	0.34	1.55	1.18

Table 2: A example verb from each of the four conditions. On the left, probabilities of complement types: noun phrase (NP), infinitive (Inf), prepositional phrase (PP), sentential complement (SC); on the right, SC surprisal and subcategorization frame entropy.

receive feedback on their responses. The experiment was conducted online using a Flash application written by Harry Tily (now at Nuance Communications).

2.2.4 Statistical analysis

Subjects were excluded if their answer accuracy was lower than 75% (two subjects), or if their mean reading time (RT) differed by more than 2.5 standard deviations from the overall mean RT across subjects (two subjects). The results reported in what follows are based on the remaining 124 subjects (97%).

We followed standard preprocessing procedure. Individual words were excluded if their raw RT was less than 100 ms or more than 2000 ms, or if the log-transformed RT was more than 3 standard deviations away from the participant's mean. Log RTs were length-corrected by taking the residuals of a mixed-effects model (Bates et al., 2012) that had log RT as the response variable, word length as a fixed effect, and a by-subject intercept and slope.

The length-corrected reading times were regressed against the predictors of interest, separately for each region. We used a maximal random effect structure. All *p* values for fixed effects were calculated using model comparison with a simpler model with the same random effect structure that did not contain that fixed effect.

2.3 Results

Reading times on the matrix subject (*the men*) or matrix verb (*discovered*) did not vary significantly across conditions.

The embedded subject *the island* was read faster in unambiguous sentences ($p < 0.001$). Reading times on this region were longer when SC surprisal was high ($p = 0.04$). Models fitted to ambiguous and unambiguous sentences separately revealed that the simple effect of SC surprisal on the embedded subject was significant for unambiguous sentences ($p = 0.02$) but not for ambiguous sentences ($p = 0.46$), though the interaction between SC surprisal and ambiguity did not reach significance ($p = 0.22$).

The embedded verb complex (*had been invaded*) was read faster in unambiguous than in ambiguous sentences ($p < 0.001$). Reading times in this region were longer overall in the high SC surprisal condition ($p = 0.03$). As expected, this effect interacted with the presence of *that* ($p = 0.01$): the simple effect of SC surprisal was not significant in unambiguous sentences ($p = 0.28$), but was highly significant in ambiguous ones ($p = 0.007$). We did not find an interaction between SC surprisal and subcategorization frame entropy (of the sort predicted by the commitment hypothesis).

Subcategorization frame entropy did not have a significant effect in any of the regions of the sentence. It was only strictly predicted to have an effect on the matrix verb: longer reading times according to the competition hypothesis, and (possibly) shorter reading times according to the commitment hypothesis. The absence of an subcategorization frame entropy effect provides weak support for the predictions of surprisal theory, according to which entropy should not affect reading times.

3 Deriving predictions from a PCFG

3.1 Calculating entropy

As mentioned above, the entropy of the next derivation step following the current word (which we term *single-step entropy*) is calculated as follows. If a_i is a nonterminal, Π_i is the set of rules rewriting a_i, and p_r is the application probability of rule r, then the single-step entropy of a_i is given by

$$h(a_i) = -\sum_{r \in \Pi_i} p_r \log_2 p_r \qquad (3)$$

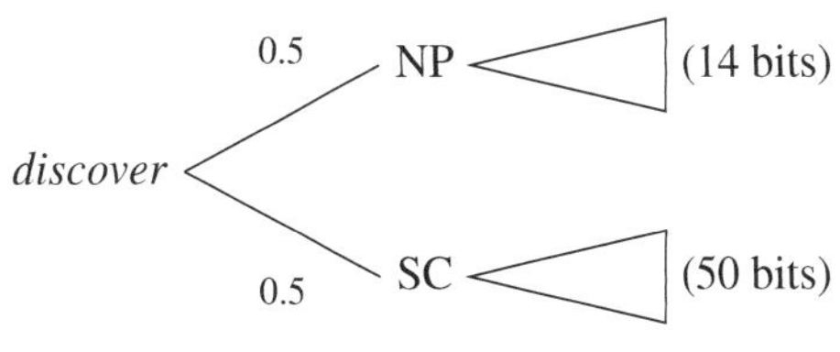

Figure 3: Entropy calculation example: the single step entropy after *discover* is 1 bit; the overall entropy is $1 + 0.5 \times 14 + 0.5 \times 50 = 33$ bits.

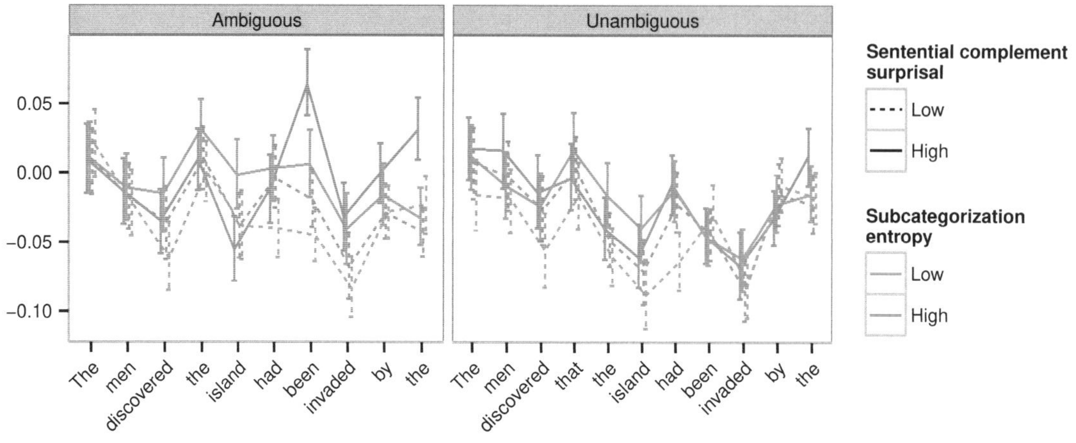

Figure 2: Results of the self-paced reading experiment

The entropy of all derivations starting with a_i (which we term *total entropy*) is then given by the following recurrence:

$$H(a_i) = h(a_i) + \sum_{r \in \Pi_i} p_r \sum_{j=1}^{k_r} H(a_{r,j}) \quad (4)$$

where $a_{r,1}, \ldots, a_{r,k_r}$ are the nonterminals on the right-hand side of r. This recurrence has a closed form solution (Wetherell, 1980; Hale, 2006). The expectation matrix A is a square matrix with N rows and columns, where N is the set of nonterminals. Each element A_{ij} indicates the expected number of times nonterminal a_j will occur when a_i is rewritten using exactly one rule of the grammar. If $h = (h_1, \ldots, h_N)$ is the vector of all single-step entropy values for the N nonterminal types in the grammar, and $H = (H_1, \ldots, H_N)$ is the vector of all total entropy values, then the closed form solution for the recurrence is given by

$$H = (I - A)^{-1} h \quad (5)$$

where I is the identity matrix. The entropy after the first n words of the sentence, H_{w_n}, can be calculated by applying Equation 5 to the grammar formed by intersecting the original grammar with the prefix $w_1, \ldots, w_n$ (i.e., considering only the parses that are compatible with the words encountered so far) (Hale, 2006).

Two points are worth noting about these equations. First, Equation 5 shows that calculating the entropy of a PCFG requires inverting the matrix $I - A$, which is the size of the number of nonterminal symbols in the grammar. This makes it impractical to use a lexicalized grammar, as advocated by Roark et al. (2009), since those grammars have a very large number of nonterminal types.

Second, Equation 4 shows that the entropy of a nonterminal is the sum of its single-step entropy and a weighted average of entropy of the nonterminals it derives. In the context of subcategorization decisions, the number of possible subcategorization frames is small, and the single-step entropy is on the order of magnitude of 1 or 2 bits. The entropy of a typical complement, on the other hand, is much higher (consider all of the possible internal structures that an SC could have). This means that the total entropy H after processing the verb is dominated by the entropy of its potential complements rather than the verb's single-step entropy h (see Figure 3 for an illustration). A lookahead of a single word (as used in Roark et al. (2009)) may therefore be only weakly related to total entropy.

3.2 Constructing the grammar

We used a PCFG induced from the Penn Treebank (Marcus et al., 1993). As mentioned above, the grammar was mostly unlexicalized; however, in order for the predictions to depend on the identity of the verb, the grammar had to contain lexically specific rules for each verb. We discuss these rules at end of this section.

The Penn Treebank tag set is often expanded by adding to each node's tag an annotation of the node's parent, e.g., marking an NP whose parent is a VP as NP_VP (Klein and Manning, 2003). While systematic parent annotation would have increased the size of the grammar dramatically, we did take the following minimal steps to improve parsing accuracy. First, the word *that* is tagged in the Penn Treebank as a preposition (IN) when it occurs as a subordinating conjunction. This resulted in SCs being erroneously parsed as prepositional phrases. To deal with this issue, we replaced the generic IN with IN[*that*] whenever it referred to *that*.

Second, the parser assigned high probability parses to reduced relative clauses in implausible contexts. We made sure that cases that should not be reduced relative clauses were not parsed as such by splitting the VP category into sub-categories based on the leftmost child of the VP (since only VP[VPN] should be able to be a reduced relative), and by splitting SBAR into SBAR[overt] when the SBAR had an overt complementizer and SBAR[none] when it did not.

Following standard practice, we removed grammatical role information and filler-gap annotations, e.g., NP-SUBJ-2 was treated as NP. To reduce the number of rules in the grammar as much as possible, we removed punctuation and the silent element NONE (used to mark gaps, silent complementizers, etc.), rules that occurred less than 100 times (out of the total 1320490 nonterminal productions), and rules that had a probability of less than 0.01. These steps resulted in the removal of 13%, 14% and 10% rule tokens respectively. We then applied horizontal Markovization (Klein and Manning, 2003).

Finally, we added lexically specific rules to capture the verbs' subcategorization preferences, based on the Gahl et al. (2004) subcategorization database. The probability of frame f_j following verb v_i was calculated as:

$$P(\text{VP[VBD]} \rightarrow v_i\ f_j) = \frac{1}{2}\frac{P(v_i)P(f_j|v_i)}{\sum_i P(v_i)} \quad (6)$$

In other words, half of the probability mass of production rules deriving VP[VBD] (VP headed by past tense verbs) was taken away from the unlexicalized rules and assigned to the verb-specific rules. The same procedure was performed for VP[VBN] (VP headed by a past participle, with the exception of the verbs *forgot* and *wrote*, which are not ambiguous between the past and past participle forms. The total probability of all rules deriving VP as a specific verb (e.g., *discovered*) was estimated as the corpus frequency of that verb divided by the total corpus frequency of all 32 verbs used in the experiment, yielding a normalized estimate of the relative frequency of that verb.

3.3 Surprisal, entropy and entropy reduction profiles

Word-by-word surprisal, entropy and entropy reduction values for each item were derived from the equations in Section 3.1 using the Cornell Conditional Probability Calculator (provided by John Hale). Figure 4 shows the predictions averaged by the conditions of the factorial design. Surprisal on the verb is always high because this is the only part of the grammar that encodes lexical identity; surprisal on the verb therefore conflates lexical and syntactic surprisal. Surprisal values on all other words are low, with the exception of the point at which the reader gets the information that the verb's complement is an SC: the embedded verb complex in ambiguous sentences, and the complementizer in unambiguous sentence.

The entropy profile is dominated by the fact that SCs have much higher internal entropy than NPs. As a consequence, entropy after the verb is higher whenever an SC is a more likely subcategorization frame. The entropy after high subcategorization frame entropy verbs is higher than that after low subcategorization frame entropy verbs, though the difference is small in comparison to the effect of SC surprisal. In ambiguous sentences, entropy remains higher for low SC surprisal verbs throughout the ambiguous region. Somewhat counterintuitively, entropy *increases* when the parse is disambiguated in favor of an SC. This is again a consequence of the higher internal entropy of a SC: the entropy of the ambiguity between SC and NP is dwarfed by the internal entropy of a SC. The entropy profile for unambiguous sentences is straightforward: it increases sharply when the reader finds out that the complement is a SC, then decreases gradually as more details are revealed about the internal structure of the SC.

The reading time predictions made by the entropy reduction hypothesis are therefore very different than those made by surprisal theory. On the verb, the entropy reduction hypothesis predicts that high SC surprisal verbs will be read more

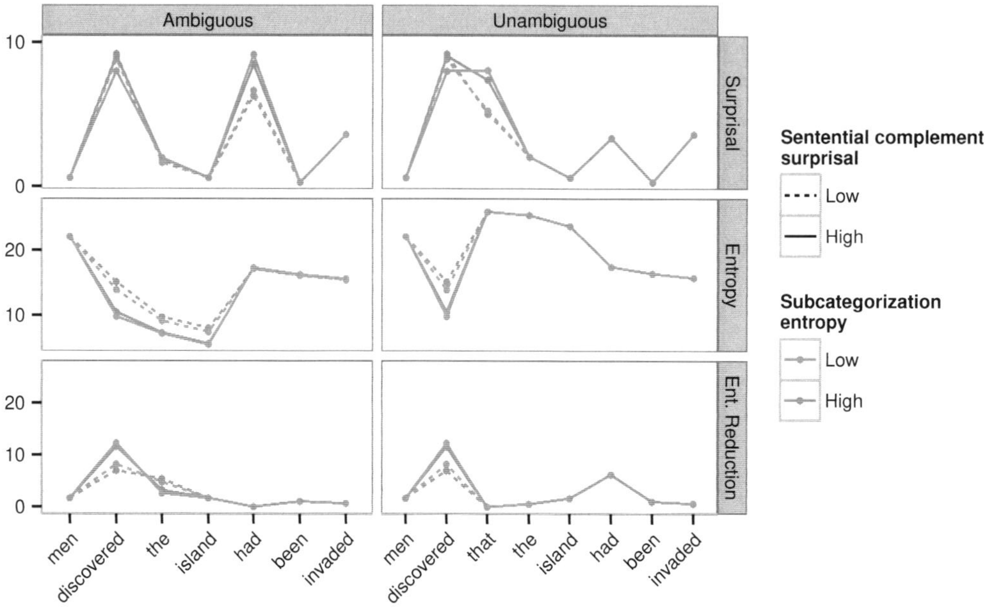

Figure 4: Parser-derived surprisal, entropy and entropy reduction estimates for the stimuli in our experiments, averaged within each condition of the factorial design (first word of sentence and *rest* region excluded).

slowly than low SC surprisal verbs, whereas surprisal predicts no difference. On the disambiguating region in ambiguous sentences, the entropy reduction hypothesis predicts no reading time differences at all, since an increase in entropy is not predicted to affect reading times. In fact, entropy reduction on the word *had* is positive only in unambiguous sentences, so the entropy reduction hypothesis predicts a slowdown in unambiguous compared to ambiguous sentences.

3.4 Evaluation on reading times

We tested whether reading times could be predicted by the word-by-word estimates derived from the PCFG. Since total entropy, entropy reduction and surprisal values did not line up with the factorial design, we used continuous regression instead, again using *lme4* with a maximal random effects structure. We only analyzed words for which the predictions depended on the properties of the verb (as Figure 4 shows, this is only the case for a minority of the words). As outcome variables, we considered both reading times on the word w_i, and a spillover variable computed as the sum of the reading times on w_i and the next word w_{i+1}. The predictors were standardized (separately for each word) to facilitate effect comparison.

Parser-derived entropy reduction values varied the most on the main verb. Since the word following the verb differs between the ambiguous and unambiguous conditions, we added a categorical control variable for sentence ambiguity. In the resulting model, lower entropy (or equivalently, higher entropy reduction values), caused an increase in reading times (no spillover: $\hat{\beta} = 0.014$, $p = 0.05$; one word spillover: $\hat{\beta} = 0.022$, $p = 0.04$). Our design does not enable us to determine whether the effect of entropy on the verb is due to entropy *reduction* or simply entropy. The commitment hypothesis is therefore equally supported by this pattern as is the entropy reduction hypothesis.

The only other word on which entropy reduction values varied across verbs was the first word *the* of the ambiguous region. Neither entropy reduction nor surprisal were significant predictors of reading times on this word.

There was also some variation across verbs in entropy (though not entropy reduction) on the second word of the embedded subject (*island*) in ambiguous sentences; however, entropy was not a significant predictor of reading times on that word. In general, entropy is much higher in the embedded subject region in unambiguous than ambiguous sentences, since it is already known that the complement is an SC, and the entropy of an SC is higher. Yet as mentioned above, reading times on the embedded subject were higher when it was ambiguous ($p < 0.001$).

Finally, PCFG-based surprisal was a significant predictor of reading times on the disambiguating word in ambiguous sentences (no spillover: *n.s.*; one word spillover: $\hat{\beta} = 0.037$, $p = 0.02$; two-word spillover: $\hat{\beta} = 0.058$, $p = 0.001$). In contrast with simple SC surprisal (see Section 2.2.4), PCFG-based surprisal was not a significant predictor of reading times on the complementizer *that* in unambiguous sentences.

4 Discussion

We presented four hypotheses as to the role of entropy in syntactic processing, and evaluated them on the results of a reading time study. We did not find significant effects of subcategorization frame entropy, which is the entropy over the next derivation step following the verb. Entropy over complete derivations, on the other hand, was a significant predictor of reading time on the verb. The effect went in the direction predicted by the entropy reduction and commitment hypotheses, and opposite to that predicted by the competition hypothesis: reading times were higher when post-verb entropy was lower.

Reading times on the embedded subject in ambiguous sentences were increased compared to unambiguous sentences. This can be seen as supporting the competition hypothesis: the SC and NP parses both need to be maintained, which increases processing cost. Yet the parser predictions showed that total entropy on the embedded subject was higher in unambiguous than ambiguous sentences, since the probability of the high-entropy sentential complement is 1 in unambiguous sentences. In this case, then, total entropy, which entails searching enormous amounts of predicted structure, may not be the right measure, and single-step (or n-step) entropy may be a better predictor.

In related work, Frank (2013) tested a version of the entropy reduction hypothesis whereby entropy reduction was not bounded by 0 (was allowed to take negative values). A Simple Recurrent Network was used to predict the next four words in the sentence; the uncertainty following the current word was estimated as the entropy of this quadrigram distribution. Higher (modified) entropy reduction resulted in increased reading times. These results are not directly comparable to the present results, however. Frank (2013) tested a theory that takes into account both positive and negative entropy changes. In addition, a four-word lookahead may not capture the dramatic difference in internal entropy between SCs and NPs, which is responsible for the differential reading times predicted on the matrix. This caveat applies even more strongly to the one-word lookahead in Roark et al. (2009).

In contrast with much previous work, we calculated total entropy using a realistic PCFG acquired from a Treebank corpus. In future work, this method can be used to investigate the effect of entropy in a naturalistic reading time corpus. It will be important to explore the extent to which the reading time predictions derived from the grammar are affected by representational decisions (e.g., the parent annotations we used in Section 3.2). This applies in particular to entropy, which is sensitive to the distribution over syntactic parses active at the word; surprisal depends only the conditional probability assigned to the word by the grammar, irrespective of the number and distribution over the parses that predict the current word, and is therefore somewhat less sensitive to representational assumptions.

5 Conclusion

This paper described four hypotheses regarding the role of uncertainty in sentence processing. A reading time study replicated a known effect of surprisal, and found a previously undocumented effect of entropy. Entropy predicted reading times only when it was calculated over complete derivations of the sentence, and not when it was calculated over the single next derivation step. Our results suggest that a full theory of sentence processing would need to take both surprisal and uncertainty into account.

Acknowledgments

We thank Alec Marantz for discussion and Andrew Watts for technical assistance. This work was supported by an Alfred P. Sloan Fellowship to T. Florian Jaeger.

References

D. Bates, M. Maechler, and B. Bolker, 2012. *lme4: Linear mixed-effects models using S4 classes*. R package version 0.999999-0.

M. Brysbaert and B. New. 2009. Moving beyond Kučera and Francis: A critical evaluation of current word frequency norms and the introduction of a new and improved word frequency measure for American English. *Behavior Research Methods*, 41(4):977–990.

V. Demberg and F. Keller. 2008. Data from eye-tracking corpora as evidence for theories of syntactic processing complexity. *Cognition*, 109(2):193–210.

K. D. Federmeier. 2007. Thinking ahead: The role and roots of prediction in language comprehension. *Psychophysiology*, 44(4):491–505.

S. L. Frank. 2013. Uncertainty reduction as a measure of cognitive load in sentence comprehension. *Topics in Cognitive Science*, 5(3):475–494.

S. Gahl, D. Jurafsky, and D. Roland. 2004. Verb subcategorization frequencies: American English corpus data, methodological studies, and cross-corpus comparisons. *Behavior Research Methods*, 36(3):432–443.

S. Garnsey, N. Pearlmutter, E. Myers, and M. Lotocky. 1997. The contributions of verb bias and plausibility to the comprehension of temporarily ambiguous sentences. *Journal of Memory and Language*, 37(1):58–93.

J. Hale. 2003. The information conveyed by words in sentences. *Journal of Psycholinguistic Research*, 32(2):101–123.

J. Hale. 2006. Uncertainty about the rest of the sentence. *Cognitive Science*, 30(4):643–672.

D. Jurafsky. 1996. A probabilistic model of lexical and syntactic access and disambiguation. *Cognitive Science*, 20(2):137–194.

D. Klein and C. D. Manning. 2003. Accurate unlexicalized parsing. In *Proceedings of the 41st Annual Meeting on Association for Computational Linguistics-Volume 1*, pages 423–430. Association for Computational Linguistics.

M. P. Marcus, M. A. Marcinkiewicz, and B. Santorini. 1993. Building a large annotated corpus of English: The Penn Treebank. *Computational Linguistics*, 19(2):313–330.

K. McRae, M. Spivey-Knowlton, and M. Tanenhaus. 1998. Modeling the influence of thematic fit (and other constraints) in on-line sentence comprehension. *Journal of Memory and Language*, 38(3):283–312.

B. Roark, A. Bachrach, C. Cardenas, and C. Pallier. 2009. Deriving lexical and syntactic expectation-based measures for psycholinguistic modeling via incremental top-down parsing. In *Proceedings of the 2009 Conference on Empirical Methods in Natural Language Processing: Volume 1-Volume 1*, pages 324–333. Association for Computational Linguistics.

N. J. Smith and R. Levy. 2013. The effect of word predictability on reading time is logarithmic. *Cognition*, 128(3):302–319.

W. Tabor and M. K. Tanenhaus. 1999. Dynamical models of sentence processing. *Cognitive Science*, 23(4):491–515.

J. Trueswell, M. Tanenhaus, and C. Kello. 1993. Verb-specific constraints in sentence processing: Separating effects of lexical preference from garden-paths. *Journal of Experimental Psychology: Learning, Memory, and Cognition*, 19(3):528–553.

C. Van Petten and B. Luka. 2012. Prediction during language comprehension: Benefits, costs, and ERP components. *International Journal of Psychophysiology*, 83(2):176–190.

C. S. Wetherell. 1980. Probabilistic languages: A review and some open questions. *ACM Computing Surveys (CSUR)*, 12(4):361–379.

J. Yun, J. Whitman, and J. Hale. 2010. Subject-object asymmetries in Korean sentence comprehension. In *Proceedings of the 32nd Annual Meeting of the Cognitive Science Society*.

Sentence Processing in a Vectorial Model of Working Memory

William Schuler
Department of Linguistics
The Ohio State University
schuler@ling.osu.edu

Abstract

This paper presents a vectorial incremental parsing model defined using independently posited operations over activation-based working memory and weight-based episodic memory. This model has the attractive property that it hypothesizes only one unary preterminal rule application and only one binary branching rule application per time step, which allows it to be smoothly integrated into a vector-based recurrence that propagates structural ambiguity from one time step to the next. Predictions of this model are calculated on a center-embedded sentence processing task and shown to exhibit decreased processing accuracy in center-embedded constructions.

1 Introduction

Current models of memory (Marr, 1971; Anderson et al., 1977; Murdock, 1982; McClelland et al., 1995; Howard and Kahana, 2002) involve a continuous *activation-based* (or 'working') memory, typically modeled as a vector representing the current firing pattern of neurons or neural clusters in the cortex. This activation-based memory is then supported by a durable but rapidly mutable *weight-based* (or 'episodic') memory, typically modeled as one or more matrices formed by summed outer-products of cue and target vectors and cued by simple matrix multiplication, representing variable synaptic connection strengths between neurons or neural clusters.

The lack of discrete memory units in such models makes it difficult to imagine a neural implementation of a typical e.g. chart-based computational account of sentence processing. On the other hand, superposition in vectorial models suggests a natural representation of a parallel incremental processing model. This paper explores how such an austere model of memory not only might be used to encode a simple probabilistic incremental parser, but also lends itself to naturally implement a vectorial interpreter and coreference resolver. This model is based on the left-corner parser formulation of van Schijndel et al. (2013a), which has the attractive property of generating exactly one binary-branching rule application after processing each word. This property greatly simplifies a vectorial implementation because it allows these single grammar rule applications to be superposed in cases of attachment ambiguity.

Predictions of the vectorial model described in this paper are then calculated on a simple center-embedded sentence processing task, producing a lower completion accuracy for center-embedded sentences than for right-branching sentences with the same number of words. As noted by Levy and Gibson (2013), this kind of memory effect is not easily explained by existing information-theoretic models of frequency effects (Hale, 2001; Levy, 2008).

The model described in this paper also provides an explanation for the apparent reality of linguistic objects like categories, grammar rules, discourse referents and dependency relations, as cognitive states in activation-based memory (in the case of categories and discourse referents), or cued associations in weight-based memory (in the case of grammar rules, and dependency relations), without having to posit complex machinery specific to language processing. In this sense, unlike existing chart-based parsers or connectionist models based on recurrent neural networks, this model integrates familiar notions of grammar and semantic relations with current ideas of activation-based and weight-based memory. It is also anticipated that this interface to both linguistic and neuroscientific theories will make the model useful as a basis for more nuanced understanding of linguistic phenomena such as ambiguity resolution, seman-

Proceedings of the 2014 ACL Workshop on Cognitive Modeling and Computational Linguistics, pages 19–27,
Baltimore, Maryland USA, June 26 2014.

tic representation, and language acquisition.

2 Related Work

The model described in this paper is based on the left-corner parser formulation of van Schijndel et al. (2013a), which is an implementation of a fully parallel incremental parser. This parser differs from chart-based fully parallel incremental parsers used by Hale (2001), Levy (2008) and others in that it enforces a cognitively-motivated bound on center-embedding depth. This bound allows the parser to represent a tractable set of incremental hypotheses in an explicitly enumerated list as a factored hidden Markov model, without necessitating the use of a parser chart. This model has the attractive property that, in any context, it hypothesizes exactly one binary-branching rule application at each time step.

The model described in this paper extends the van Schijndel et al. (2013a) parser by maintaining possible store configurations as superposed sequence states in a finite-dimensional state vector. The model then exploits the uniformity of its parsing operations to integrate probabilistically weighted grammar rule applications into this superposed state vector. These superposed states are then used to cue more superordinate sequential states as 'continuations' whenever subordinate states conclude. Interference in this cueing process is then observed to produce a natural center-embedding limit.

This model is defined as a recurrence over an activation vector, similar to the simple recurrent network of Elman (1991) and others, but unlike an SRN, which does not encode anything in weight-based memory during processing, this model encodes updates to a processing hierarchy in weight-based memory at every time step. The model is also similar to the ACT-R parser of Lewis and Vasishth (2005) in that it maintains a single state which is updated based on content-based cued association, but unlike the ACT-R parser, which cues category tokens on category types and therefore models memory limits as interference among grammar rules, this model cues category tokens on other category tokens, and therefore predicts memory limits even in cases where grammar rules do not involve similar category types. Also unlike Lewis and Vasishth (2005), this model is defined purely in terms of state vectors and outer-product associative memory and therefore has the capacity to maintain parallel states in superposition.

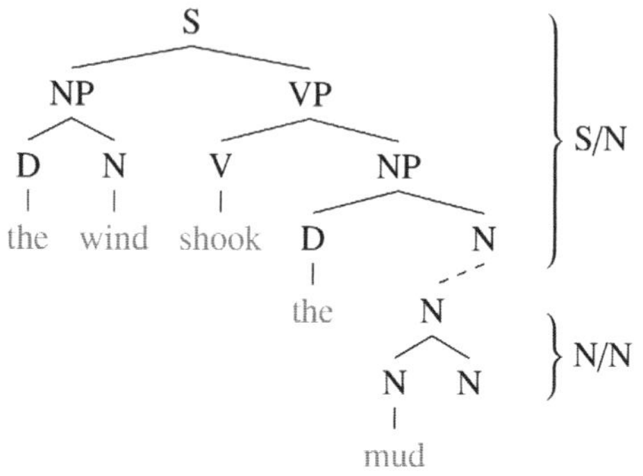

Figure 1: Example incomplete category during processing of the sentence *The wind shook the mud room door.*

3 Background: Non-vectorial Incremental Parsing

The model defined in this paper is based on the left-corner parser formulation of van Schijndel et al. (2013a). This parser maintains a set of incomplete categories a/b at each time step, each consisting of an active category a lacking an awaited category b yet to come. For example, Figure 1 shows an incomplete category S/N consisting of a sentence lacking a common noun yet to come, which non-immediately dominates another incomplete category N/N consisting of a common noun lacking another common noun yet to come.

Processing in this model is defined to alternate between two phases:

1. a 'fork' phase in which a word is either used to complete an existing incomplete category, or forked into a new complete category; and
2. a 'join' phase in which one of these complete categories is used as a left child of a grammar rule application and then either joined onto a superordinate incomplete category or kept disjoint.

In any case, only one grammar rule is applied after each word. These fork and join operations are shown graphically and as natural deduction rules in Figure 2.

An example derivation of the sentence, *The wind shook the mud room door*, using the productions in Figure 2 is shown in Figure 3, with corresponding partial parse trees shown in Figure 4. Van Schijndel et al. (2013a) show that a

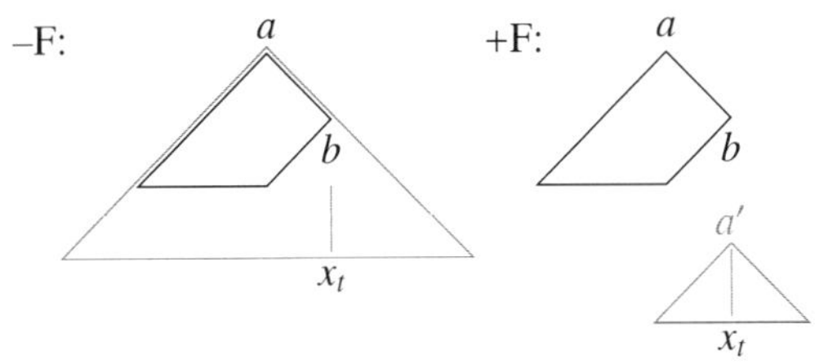

$$\frac{a/b \quad x_t}{a}\; b \rightarrow x_t \qquad (\text{–F})$$

$$\frac{a/b \quad x_t}{a/b \quad a'}\; b \xrightarrow{+} a' \ldots ;\; a' \rightarrow x_t \qquad (\text{+F})$$

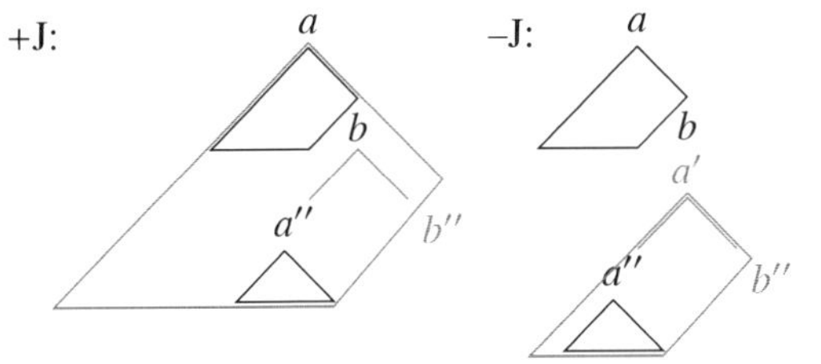

$$\frac{a/b \quad a''}{a/b''}\; b \rightarrow a''\; b'' \qquad (\text{+J})$$

$$\frac{a/b \quad a''}{a/b \quad a'/b''}\; b \xrightarrow{+} a' \ldots ;\; a' \rightarrow a''\; b'' \qquad (\text{–J})$$

Figure 2: Fork and join operations from the van Schijndel et al. (2013a) left-corner parser formulation. During the fork phase, word x either completes an existing incomplete category a, or forks into a new complete category a'. During the join phase, complete category a'' becomes a left child of a grammar rule application, then either joins onto a superordinate incomplete category a/b or remains disjoint.

probabilistic version of this incremental parser can reproduce the results of a state-of-the-art chart-based parser (Petrov and Klein, 2007).

4 Vectorial Parsing

This left corner parser can be implemented in a vectorial model of working memory using vectors as activation-based memory and matrices as weight-based memory. Following Anderson et al. (1977) and others, vectors v in activation-based memory are cued from other vectors u through weight-based memory matrices M using ordinary

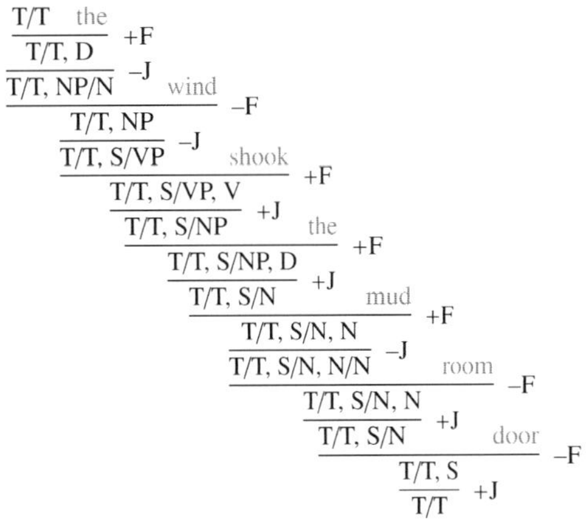

Figure 3: Processing steps in parsing the sentence *The wind shook the mud room door.*

matrix multiplication:[1]

$$v = M\,u \qquad (1)$$

This representation has been used to model the influence of activation in antecedent neurons on activation in consequent neurons (Marr, 1971; Anderson et al., 1977).

Unless they are cued from some other source, all vectors in this model are initially randomly generated by sampling from an exponential distribution, denoted here simply by:

$$v \sim \text{Exp} \qquad (2)$$

Also following Anderson et al. (1977), weight-based memory matrices M are themselves defined and updated by simply adding outer products of desired cue u and target v vectors:[2]

$$M_t = M_{t-1} + v \otimes u \qquad (3)$$

This representation has been used to model rapid synaptic sensitization in the hippocampus (Marr, 1971; McClelland et al., 1995), in which synapses of activated antecedent neurons that impinge on activated consequent neurons are strengthened.

[1] That is, multiplication of an associative memory matrix M by a state vector v yields:

$$(M\,v)_{[i]} \stackrel{\text{def}}{=} \textstyle\sum_{j=1}^{J} M_{[i,j]} \cdot v_{[j]} \qquad (1')$$

[2] An outer product $v \otimes u$ defines a matrix by multiplying each combination of scalars in vectors v and u:

$$(v \otimes u)_{[j,i]} \stackrel{\text{def}}{=} v_{[j]} \cdot u_{[i]} \qquad (2')$$

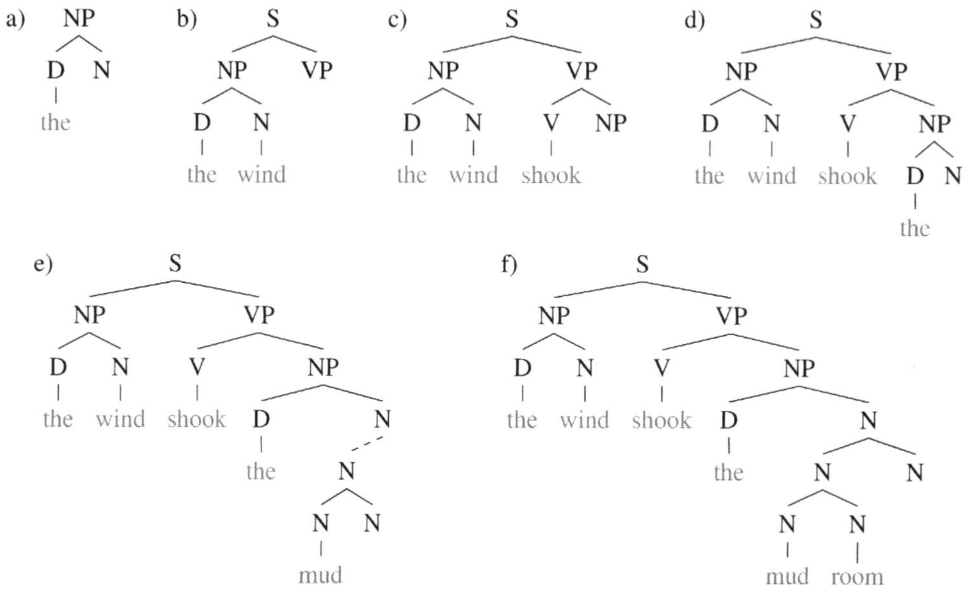

Figure 4: Processing steps in parsing the sentence *The wind shook the mud room door.*

Finally, cued associations can be combined using pointwise or diagonal products:[3]

$$w = \mathrm{diag}(u)\, v \tag{4}$$

Unlike a symbolic statistical model, a vectorial model must explicitly distinguish token representations from types in order to define structural relations that would be implicit in the positions of data structure elements in a symbolic model. Thus, the active or awaited distinction is applied to category tokens rather than types, but grammar rule applications are defined over category types rather than tokens.

The vectorial left-corner parser described in this paper is therefore defined on a single category token vector b_t which encodes the awaited category token of the most subordinate incomplete category at the current time step t. A hierarchy of nested incomplete category tokens is then encoded in two 'continuation' matrices:

- A_t, which cues the active category token a of the same incomplete category as a given awaited token b; and
- B_t, which cues the awaited category token b of the incomplete category that non-immediately dominates any active category token a.

Together, the cued associations in these continuation matrices trace a path up from the most subordinate awaited category token b to the most superordinate category token currently hypothesized as the root of the syntactic tree. Vectors for category types c can then be cued from any category token a or b through an associative matrix C_t. All three of these matrices may be updated from time step to time step by associating cue and target vectors through outer product addition, as described above.

The model also defines vectors for binary-branching grammar rules g, which are associated with parent, left child, or right child category types via 'accessor' matrices G, G', or G''.[4] These accessor matrices are populated from binary-branching rules in a probabilistic context-free grammar (PCFG) in Chomsky Normal Form (CNF). For example, the PCFG rule $\mathsf{P}(\mathrm{S} \rightarrow \mathrm{NP\ VP}) = 0.8$ may be encoded using a

[3] A diagonal product $\mathrm{diag}(v)\, u$ defines a vector by multiplying corresponding scalars in vectors v and u:

$$(\mathrm{diag}(v)\, u)_{[i]} \stackrel{\mathrm{def}}{=} v_{[i]} \cdot u_{[i]} \tag{3'}$$

[4] This use of reification and accessor matrices for grammar rules emulates a tensor model (Smolensky, 1990; beim Graben et al., 2008) in that in the worst case grammar rules (composed of multiple categories) would require a space polynomially larger than that of category types, but since this space is sparsely inhabited in the expected case, this reified representation is computationally more tractable.

grammar rule vector $g_{\text{S} \rightarrow \text{NP VP}}$ and category vectors $c_{\text{S}}, c_{\text{VP}}, c_{\text{NP}}$ with the following outer-product associations:

$$G \stackrel{\text{def}}{=} g_{\text{S} \rightarrow \text{NP VP}} \otimes c_{\text{S}} \cdot 0.8$$

$$G' \stackrel{\text{def}}{=} g_{\text{S} \rightarrow \text{NP VP}} \otimes c_{\text{NP}}$$

$$G'' \stackrel{\text{def}}{=} g_{\text{S} \rightarrow \text{NP VP}} \otimes c_{\text{VP}}$$

Grammars with additional rules can then be encoded as a sum of outer products of rule and category vectors. Grammar rules can then be cued from category types by matrix multiplication, e.g.:

$$g_{\text{S} \rightarrow \text{NP VP}} = G'\, c_{\text{NP}}$$

and category types can be cued from grammar rules using transposed versions of accessor matrices:

$$c_{\text{NP}} = G'^{\top} g_{\text{S} \rightarrow \text{NP VP}}$$

The model also defines:

- vectors x_t for observation types (i.e. words),
- a matrix P cueing category types from observation types, populated from unary rules in a CNF PCFG, and
- a matrix $D = D_K$ of leftmost descendant categories cued from ancestor categories, derived from accessor matrices G and G' by K iterations of the following recurrence:[5]

$$D'_0 \stackrel{\text{def}}{=} \text{diag}(\mathbf{1}) \tag{5}$$

$$D_0 \stackrel{\text{def}}{=} \text{diag}(\mathbf{0}) \tag{6}$$

$$D'_k \stackrel{\text{def}}{=} G'^{\top}\, G\, D'_{k\text{-}1} \tag{7}$$

$$D_k \stackrel{\text{def}}{=} D_{k\text{-}1} + D'_k \tag{8}$$

  where each D'_k cues a probabilistically-weighted descendant at distance k from its cue, and D_k is the superposition of all such descendant associations from length 1 to length K. This produces a superposed set of category types that may occur as leftmost descendants of a (possibly superposed) ancestor category type.

In order to exclude active category types $C_t\, a_t$ that are not compatible with awaited category types $C_t\, b_t$ in the same incomplete category, the model also defines:

- a matrix $E = E_K$ of rightmost descendant categories cued from ancestor categories, derived in the same manner as D, except using G'' in place of G'.

The parser proceeds in two phases, generating a complete category token vector a''_t from $b_{t\text{-}1}$ during the F phase, then generating an awaited category token vector b_t of an incomplete category during the J phase. Since the parser proceeds in two phases, this paper will distinguish variables updated in each phase using a subscript for time step $t-.5$ at the end of the first phase and t at the end of the second phase.

The vectorial parser implements the F phase of the left-corner parser (the 'fork/no-fork' decision) by first defining two new category tokens for the possibly forked or unforked complete category:

$$a_{t\text{-}.5},\ a'_{t\text{-}.5} \sim \text{Exp}$$

The parser then obtains:

- the category type of the most subordinate awaited category token at the previous time step: $C_{t\text{-}1}\, b_{t\text{-}1}$ (which involves no fork), and
- a superposed set of non-immediate descendants of the category type of this most subordinate awaited category token: $D\, C_{t\text{-}1}\, b_{t\text{-}1}$ (which involves a fork),

These fork and no-fork categories are then diagonally multiplied (intersected) with a superposed set of preterminal categories for the current observation ($P\, x_t$):

$$c^{-}_t = \text{diag}(P\, x_t)\, C_{t\text{-}1}\, b_{t\text{-}1}$$

$$c^{+}_t = \text{diag}(P\, x_t)\, D\, C_{t\text{-}1}\, b_{t\text{-}1}$$

The B and C continuation and category matrices are then updated with a superordinate awaited category token and category type for a and a':

$$a_{t\text{-}1} = A_{t\text{-}1}\, b_{t\text{-}1}$$

$$B_{t\text{-}.5} = B_{t\text{-}1} + b_{t\text{-}1} \otimes a'_{t\text{-}.5} + B_{t\text{-}1}\, a_{t\text{-}1} \otimes a_{t\text{-}.5}$$

$$C_{t\text{-}.5} = C_{t\text{-}1} + c^{+}_t \otimes a'_{t\text{-}.5} + \text{diag}(C_{t\text{-}1}\, a_{t\text{-}1})\, E^{\top} c^{-}_t \otimes a_{t\text{-}.5}$$

where the updated category for $a_{t\text{-}.5}$ results from an intersection (diagonal product) of the current category at $a_{t\text{-}1}$ with the set of categories that can occur with c^{-}_t as a rightmost child, as defined by E. The intersected fork and no-fork category types are then used to weight superposed hypotheses for

[5] Here $\mathbf{1}$ and $\mathbf{0}$ denote vectors of ones and zeros, respectively.

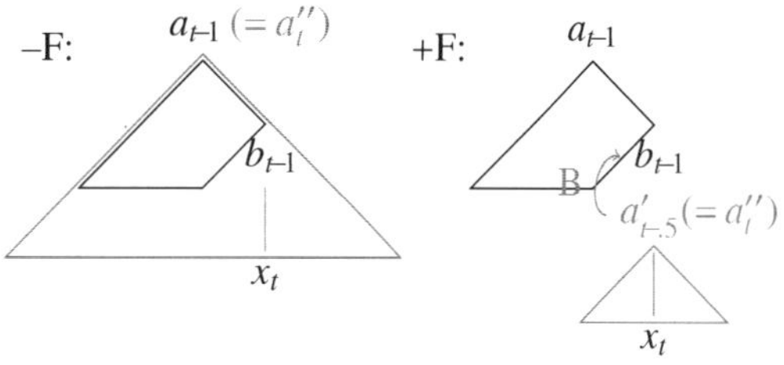

Figure 5: Updates to continuation matrices during the 'fork' phase of a left-corner parser.

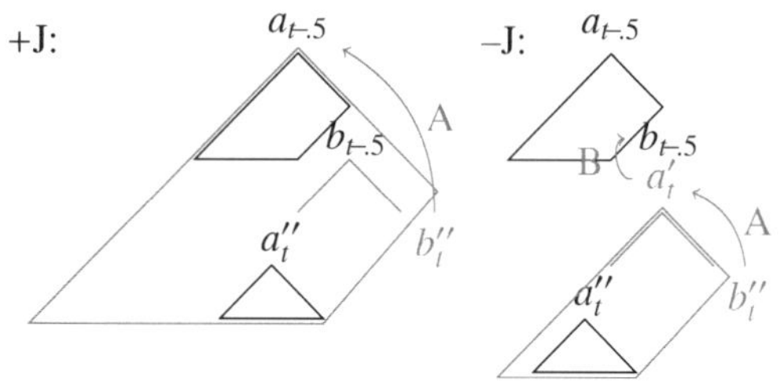

Figure 6: Updates to continuation matrices during the 'join' phase of a left-corner parser.

the complete category token a''_t that will result from this phase of processing, and the b vector is updated to encode the category token:[6]

$$a''_t = \frac{a_{t-1}\,\|c^-_t\| + a'_{t-.5}\,\|c^+_t\|}{\|a_{t-1}\,\|c^-_t\| + a'_{t-.5}\,\|c^+_t\|\|}$$
$$b_{t-.5} = B_{t-.5}\,a''_t$$

These updates can be represented graphically as shown in Figure 5.

The vectorial parser then similarly implements the J phase (the 'join/no-join' decision) of the left-corner parser by first defining a new category token a' for a possible new active category of the most subordinate incomplete category, and b'' for a new awaited category token:

$$a'_t,\ b''_t \sim \text{Exp}$$

The parser then obtains:

- a superposed set of grammar rules with parent category matching the category of the most subordinate awaited category token at the previous time step: $G\,C_{t-.5}\,b_{t-.5}$ (which assumes a join), and
- a superposed set of grammar rules with parent category non-immediately descended from the category of this most subordinate awaited category token: $G\,D\,C_{t-.5}\,b_{t-.5}$ (which assumes no join)

These join and no-join grammar rule vectors are then diagonally multiplied (intersected) with the superposed set of grammar rules whose left child category type matches the category type of the most subordinate complete category token ($G'\,C_{t-.5}\,a''_t$):

$$g^+_t = \text{diag}(G'\,C_{t-.5}\,a''_t)\,G\,C_{t-.5}\,b_{t-.5}$$
$$g^-_t = \text{diag}(G'\,C_{t-.5}\,a''_t)\,G\,D\,C_{t-.5}\,b_{t-.5}$$

These intersected join and no-join grammar rule vectors are then used to weight superposed hypotheses for the incomplete category that will result from this phase of processing in updates to the continuation and category matrices A, B, and C:

$$A_t = A_{t-1} + \frac{A_{t-1}\,b_{t-.5}\,\|g^+_t\| + a'_t\,\|g^-_t\|}{\|A_{t-1}\,b_{t-.5}\,\|g^+_t\| + a'_t\,\|g^-_t\|\|} \otimes b''_t$$
$$B_t = B_{t-.5} + b_{t-.5} \otimes a'_t$$
$$C_t = C_{t-.5} + G^{\top}g^-_t \otimes a'_t + \frac{G''^{\top}g^+_t + G''^{\top}g^-_t}{\|G''^{\top}g^+_t + G''^{\top}g^-_t\|} \otimes b''_t$$

These updates can be represented graphically as shown in Figure 6. Finally the the most subordinate awaited category token is updated for the next word:

$$b_t = b''_t$$

5 Predictions

In order to assess the cognitive plausibility of the memory modeling assumptions in this vectorial parser, predictions of the implementation defined in Section 4 were calculated on center-embedding and right-branching sentences, exemplified by:

(1) *If either Kim stays or Kim leaves then Pat leaves.* (center-embedded condition)

(2) *If Kim stays then if Kim leaves then Pat leaves.* (right-branching condition)

[6]This uses the two norm $\|v\|$, which is the magnitude of vector v, defined as the square root of the sum of the squares of its scalar values:

$$\|v\| \stackrel{\text{def}}{=} \sqrt{\textstyle\sum_i (v_{[i]})^2} \qquad (4')$$

Dividing a vector by its two norm has the effect of normalizing it to unit length.

$$P(T \rightarrow S\ T) = 1.0$$
$$P(S \rightarrow NP\ VP) = 0.5$$
$$P(S \rightarrow IF\ S\ THEN\ S) = 0.25$$
$$P(S \rightarrow EITHER\ S\ OR\ S) = 0.25$$
$$P(IF \rightarrow if) = 1.0$$
$$P(THEN \rightarrow then) = 1.0$$
$$P(EITHER \rightarrow either) = 1.0$$
$$P(OR \rightarrow or) = 1.0$$
$$P(NP \rightarrow kim) = 0.5$$
$$P(NP \rightarrow pat) = 0.5$$
$$P(VP \rightarrow leaves) = 0.5$$
$$P(VP \rightarrow stays) = 0.5$$

Figure 7: 'If ... then ...' grammar used in sentence processing experiment. Branches with arity greater than two are decomposed into equivalent right-branching sequences of binary branches.

both of which contain the same number of words. These sentences were processed using the grammar shown in Figure 7, which assigns the same probability to both center-embedding and right-branching sentences. The *if ... then ...* and *either ... or ...* constructions used in these examples are taken from the original Chomsky and Miller (1963) paper introducing center-embedding effects, and are interesting because they do not involve the same grammar rule (as is the case with familiar nested object relative constructions), and do not involve filler-gap constructions, which may introduce overhead processing costs as a possible confound.

This assessment consisted of 500 trials for each sentence type. Sentences were input to an implementation of this model using the Numpy package in Python, which consists of the equations shown in Section 4 enclosed in a loop over the words in each sentence. Each trial initially sampled a, b, c, and g vectors from random exponential distributions of dimension 100, and the parser initialized b_0 with category type T as shown in Figure 3, with the active category token at $A_0\, b_0$ also associated with category type T.

Accuracy for this assessment was calculated by finding the category type with the maximum cosine similarity for the awaited category b_T at the end of the sentence. If this category type was T

sentence	correct	incorrect
center-embedded	231	269
right-branching	297	203

Table 1: Accuracy of vectorial parser on each sentence type.

(as it is in Figure 3), the parser was awarded a point of accuracy; otherwise it was not. The results of this assessment are shown in Table 1. The parser processes sentences with right-branching structure substantially more accurately than sentences with center-embedded structure. These results are strongly significant ($p < .001$) using a χ^2 test.

These predictions seem to be consistent with observations by Chomsky and Miller (1963) that center-embedded structures are more difficult to parse than right-branching structures, but it is also important to note how the model arrives at these predictions. The decreased accuracy of center-embedded sentences is not a result of an explicit decay factor, as in ACT-R and other models (Lewis and Vasishth, 2005), or distance measures as in DLT (Gibson, 2000), nor is it attributable to cue interference (as modeled by Lewis and Vasishth for nested object relative constructions), since the inner and outer embeddings in these sentences use different grammar rules. The decreased accuracy for center-embedding is also not attributable to frequency effects of grammar rules (as modeled by Hale, 2001), since the rules in this grammar are relatively common and equally weighted.

Instead, the decrease for center-embedded structures emerges from this model as a necessary result of drift due to repeated superposition of targets encoded in continuation matrices A and B. This produces a natural decay over time as sequences of subordinate category token vectors b_t introduce noise in updates to A_t and B_t. When these matrices are cued in concert, as happens when cueing across incomplete categories, the distortion is magnified. This decay is therefore a consequence of encoding hierarchic structural information using cued associations. In contrast, right-branching parses are not similarly as badly degraded over time because the flat treatment of left- and right- branching structures in a left-corner parser does not cue as often across incomplete categories using matrix B.

6 Extensions

This model is also interesting because it allows semantic relations to be constructed using the same outer product associations used to define continuation and category matrices in Section 4. First, discourse referent instances and numbered relation types are defined as vectors i and n, respectively. Then relation tokens are reified as vectors r, similar to the reification of grammar rules described in Section 4, and connected to relation type vectors n by cued association R and to source and target discourse referents i by cued associations R' and R''. Semantic relation types can then be cued from grammar rules g using associative matrix N, allowing relations of various types to be constructed in cases of superposed grammar rules. In future work, it would be interesting to see whether this representation is consistent with observations of local syntactic coherence (Tabor et al., 2004).

This model can also constrain relations to discourse referents introduced in a previous sentence or earlier in the same sentence using a vector of *temporal features* (Howard and Kahana, 2002). This is a vector of features z_t, that has a randomly chosen selection of features randomly resampled at each time step, exponentially decreasing the cosine similarity of the current version of the z_t vector to earlier versions $z_{t'}$. If discourse referents i are cued from the current temporal features z_t in an outer product associative matrix Z, it will cue relatively recently mentioned discourse referents more strongly than less recently mentioned referents. If discourse referents for eventualities and propositions j are connected to explicit predicate type referents k (say, cued by a relation of type '0'), and if temporal cues are combined in a diagonal product with cues by semantic relations from a common predicate type, the search for a consistent discourse referent can be further constrained to match the gender of a pronoun or other relations from a definite reference. In future work, it would be interesting to compare the predictions of this kind of model to human coreference resolution, particularly in the case of parsing conjunctions with reflexive pronouns, which has been used to argue for fully connected incremental parsing (Sturt and Lombardo, 2005).

7 Conclusion

This paper has presented a vectorial left-corner parsing model defined using independently posited operations over activation-based working memory and weight-based episodic memory. This model has the attractive property that it hypothesizes only one unary branching rule application and only one binary branching rule application per time step, which allows it to be smoothly integrated into a vector-based recurrence that propagates structural ambiguity from one time step to the next. Predictions of this model were calculated on a center-embedded sentence processing task and the model was shown to exhibit decreased processing accuracy in center-embedded constructions, as observed by Chomsky and Miller (1963), even in the absence of repeated grammar rules or potential confounding overhead costs that may be associated with filler-gap constructions.

This model is particularly interesting because, unlike other vectorial or connectionist parsers, it directly implements a recursive probabilistic grammar with explicit categories of syntactic context. This explicit implementation of a probabilistic grammar allows variations of this processing model to be evaluated without having to also posit a human-like model of acquisition. For example, the model can simply be defined with a PCFG derived from a syntactically annotated corpus.

The model is also interesting because it serves as an existence proof that recursive grammar is not incompatible with current models of human memory.

Finally, the fact that this model predicts memory effects at boundaries between incomplete categories, in line with predictions of fully parallel left-corner parsers (van Schijndel and Schuler, 2013; van Schijndel et al., 2013b), suggests that measures based on incomplete categories (or based on connected components of other kinds of syntactic or semantic structure) are not simply arbitrary but rather may naturally emerge from the use of associative memory during sentence processing.

Although the model may not scale to broad-coverage parsing evaluations in its present form, future work will explore hybridization of some of these methods into a parser with an explicit beam of parallel hypotheses. It is anticipated that an algorithmic-level comprehension model such as this will allow a more nuanced understanding of human semantic representation and grammar acquisition.

References

James A. Anderson, Jack W. Silverstein, Stephen A. Ritz, and Randall S. Jones. 1977. Distinctive features, categorical perception and probability learning: Some applications of a neural model. *Psychological Review*, 84:413–451.

Peter beim Graben, Sabrina Gerth, and Shravan Vasishth. 2008. Towards dynamical system models of language-related brain potentials. *Cognitive Neurodynamics*, 2(3):229–255.

Noam Chomsky and George A. Miller. 1963. Introduction to the formal analysis of natural languages. In *Handbook of Mathematical Psychology*, pages 269–321. Wiley, New York, NY.

Jeffrey L. Elman. 1991. Distributed representations, simple recurrent networks, and grammatical structure. *Machine Learning*, 7:195–225.

Edward Gibson. 2000. The dependency locality theory: A distance-based theory of linguistic complexity. In *Image, language, brain: Papers from the first mind articulation project symposium*, pages 95–126, Cambridge, MA. MIT Press.

John Hale. 2001. A probabilistic earley parser as a psycholinguistic model. In *Proceedings of the second meeting of the North American chapter of the Association for Computational Linguistics*, pages 159–166, Pittsburgh, PA.

Marc W. Howard and Michael J. Kahana. 2002. A distributed representation of temporal context. *Journal of Mathematical Psychology*, 45:269–299.

Roger Levy and Edward Gibson. 2013. Surprisal, the pdc, and the primary locus of processing difficulty in relative clauses. *Frontiers in Psychology*, 4(229).

Roger Levy. 2008. Expectation-based syntactic comprehension. *Cognition*, 106(3):1126–1177.

Richard L. Lewis and Shravan Vasishth. 2005. An activation-based model of sentence processing as skilled memory retrieval. *Cognitive Science*, 29(3):375–419.

David Marr. 1971. Simple memory: A theory for archicortex. *Philosophical Transactions of the Royal Society (London) B*, 262:23–81.

J. L. McClelland, B. L. McNaughton, and R. C. O'Reilly. 1995. Why there are complementary learning systems in the hippocampus and neocortex: Insights from the successes and failures of connectionist models of learning and memory. *Psychological Review*, 102:419–457.

B.B. Murdock. 1982. A theory for the storage and retrieval of item and associative information. *Psychological Review*, 89:609–626.

Slav Petrov and Dan Klein. 2007. Improved inference for unlexicalized parsing. In *Proceedings of NAACL HLT 2007*, pages 404–411, Rochester, New York, April. Association for Computational Linguistics.

Paul Smolensky. 1990. Tensor product variable binding and the representation of symbolic structures in connectionist systems. *Artificial intelligence*, 46(1-2):159–216.

Patrick Sturt and Vincent Lombardo. 2005. Processing coordinate structures: Incrementality and connectedness. *Cognitive Science*, 29:291–305.

W. Tabor, B. Galantucci, and D Richardson. 2004. Effects of merely local syntactic coherence on sentence processing. *Journal of Memory and Language*, 50(4):355–370.

Marten van Schijndel and William Schuler. 2013. An analysis of frequency- and recency-based processing costs. In *Proceedings of NAACL-HLT 2013*. Association for Computational Linguistics.

Marten van Schijndel, Andy Exley, and William Schuler. 2013a. A model of language processing as hierarchic sequential prediction. *Topics in Cognitive Science*, 5(3):522–540.

Marten van Schijndel, Luan Nguyen, and William Schuler. 2013b. An analysis of memory-based processing costs using incremental deep syntactic dependency parsing. In *Proceedings of CMCL 2013*. Association for Computational Linguistics.

Evaluating Evaluation Metrics for Minimalist Parsing

Thomas Graf
Department of Linguistics
Stony Brook University
mail@thomasgraf.net

Bradley Marcinek
Department of Linguistics
Stony Brook University
bradley.marcinek@stonybrook.edu

Abstract

In response to Kobele et al. (2012), we evaluate four ways of linking the processing difficulty of sentences to the behavior of the top-down parser for Minimalist grammars developed in Stabler (2012). We investigate the predictions these four metrics make for a number of relative clause constructions, and we conclude that at this point, none of them capture the full range of attested patterns.

1 Introduction

Minimalist grammars (MGs; (Stabler, 1997)) are a mildly context-sensitive formalism inspired by Minimalist syntax (Chomsky, 1995), the dominant theory in generative syntax. MGs allow us to evaluate syntactic proposals with respect to computational and cognitive criteria such as generative capacity (Harkema, 2001; Michaelis, 2001) or the memory structures they require (Kobele et al., 2007; Graf, 2012).

A new kind of top-down parser for MGs has recently been presented by Stabler (2011b; 2012). Stabler's parser is noteworthy because it uses derivation trees as a data structure in order to reduce MG parsing to a special case of parsing context-free grammars (CFGs). This raises the question, though, whether derivation trees are a psychologically plausible data structure, and if so, to which extent the Stabler parser makes it possible to test the psycholinguistic predictions of competing syntactic analyses.

In order to address this question, a linking hypothesis is needed that connects the behavior of the parser to a processing difficulty metric. Kobele et al. (2012) — henceforth KGH — propose that the difficulty of sentence s correlates with the maximum number of parse steps the parser has to keep a parse item in memory while processing s. This metric is called *maximum tenure* (**Max**). **Max** is appealing because of its simplicity and sensitivity to differences in linguistic analysis, which makes it easy to determine the psycholinguistic predictions of a specific syntactic analyses.

In this paper, we show that **Max** does not make the right predictions for I) relative clauses embedded in a sentential complement and II) subjects gaps versus object gaps in relative clauses. We present a number of simple alternative measures that handle these phenomena correctly, but we also show that these metrics fail in other cases (all results are summarized in Tab. 1 on page 8). We conclude that the prospect of a simple direct link between syntactic analysis and processing difficulty is tempting but not sufficiently developed at this point.

The paper starts with a quick introduction to MGs (Sec. 2.1) and how they are parsed (Sec. 2.2). Section 3 then introduces three alternatives to **Max**. **Max** is then shown to fare worse than those three with respect to well-known contrasts involving relative clauses (Sec. 4). Section 5 briefly looks at three other constructions that pose problems for the alternative metrics.

2 Preliminaries

2.1 Minimalist Grammars

MGs (Stabler, 1997; Stabler, 2011a) are a highly lexicalized formalism in which structures are built via the operations Merge and Move. Intuitively, Merge enforces local dependencies via subcategorization, whereas Move establishes long-distance filler-gap dependencies.

Every lexical item comes with a non-empty list of unchecked features, and each feature has either positive or negative polarity and is checked by either Merge or Move. Suppose that I) s is a tree whose head has a positive Merge feature F^+ as its first unchecked feature, and II) t is a tree whose head has a matching negative Merge feature F^-

Proceedings of the 2014 ACL Workshop on Cognitive Modeling and Computational Linguistics, pages 28–36,
Baltimore, Maryland USA, June 26 2014. ©2014 Association for Computational Linguistics

as its first unchecked feature. Then Merge checks F^+ and F^- and combines s and t into the tree $l(s,t)$ or $l(t,s)$, where l is a label projected by the head of s and s is linearized to the left of t iff s consists of exactly one node. Move, on the other hand, applies to a single tree s whose head h has a positive Move feature f^+ as its first unchecked feature. Suppose that t is a subtree of s whose head has the matching negative Move feature f^- as its first unchecked feature. Then Move checks f^+ and f^- and returns the tree $l(t,s')$, where l is a label projected by h and s' is obtained by removing t from s. Crucially, Move may apply to s iff there is exactly one subtree like t. This restriction is known as the Shortest Move Constraint (SMC).

For example, the sentence *John left* involves (at least) the following steps under a simplified Minimalist analysis (Adger, 2003):

$$\text{Merge}(\text{John} :: \text{D}^- \ \text{nom}^-, \text{left} :: \text{D}^+ \ \text{V}^-) \\ = [_{\text{VP}} \text{ left} :: \text{V}^- \ \text{John} :: \text{nom}^- \ ] \quad (1)$$

$$\text{Merge}(\varepsilon :: \text{V}^+ \ \text{nom}^+ \ \text{T}^-, (1)) \\ = [_{\text{TP}} \ \varepsilon :: \text{nom}^+ \ \text{T}^- [_{\text{VP}} \text{ left} \\ \text{John} :: \text{nom}^-] \ ] \quad (2)$$

$$\text{Move}((2)) = [_{\text{TP}} \text{ John } [_{\text{T}'} \ \varepsilon :: \text{T}^- \\ [_{\text{VP}} \text{ left} \ ] \ ] \ ] \quad (3)$$

This derivation can be represented more succinctly as the *derivation tree* in Fig 1, where all leaves are labeled by lexical items while unary and binary branching nodes are labeled Move and Merge, respectively.

Even though MGs (with the SMC) are weakly equivalent to MCFGs (Michaelis, 2001) and thus mildly context-sensitive in the sense of Joshi (1985), their derivation tree languages can be generated by CFGs (modulo relabeling of interior nodes). As we will see next, this makes it possible to treat MG parsing as a special case of CFG parsing.

2.2 Parsing Minimalist Grammars

Thanks to the SMC, the mapping from derivation trees to phrase structure trees is deterministic. Consequently, MG parsing reduces to assigning context-free derivation trees to input sentences, rather than the more complex phrase structure trees. The major difference from CFGs is that the linear order of nodes in an MG derivation tree does not necessarily match the linear order of words in the input sentence — for instance because a moving phrase remains in its base position in the derivation tree. But as long as one can tell for every MG operation how its output is linearized, these discrepancies in linear order can be taken care of in the inference rules of the parser. Stabler (2011b; 2012) shows how exactly this is done for a parser that constructs derivation trees in a top-down fashion. Intuitively, MG top-down parsing is CFG top-down parsing with a slightly different algorithm for traversing/expanding the tree.

Instead of presenting the parser's full set of inference rules, we adopt KGH's index notation to indicate how the parser constructs a given derivation. For instance, if a derivation contains the node ${}^5\text{Merge}_{38}$, this means that the parser makes a prediction at step 5 that Merge occurs at this position in the derivation and keeps this prediction in memory until step 38, at which point the parser replaces it by suitable predictions for the arguments for Merge, i.e. the daughters of the Merge node. Similarly, ${}^{22}\text{the} :: \text{N}^+ \ \text{D}^-{}_{28}$ denotes that the parser conjectures this lexical item at step 22 and finally gets to scan it in the input string at step 28.

In principle the parser could simply predict a complete derivation and then scan the input string to see if the two match. In order to obtain an incremental parser, however, scanning steps have to take place as soon as possible. The MG parser implements this as follows: predictions are put into a priority queue, and the prediction with the highest priority is worked on first. The priority of the predictions corresponds to the linear order that holds between the constituents that are obtained from them. For example, if the parser replaces a prediction for a Merge node yielding $l(s,t)$ by predictions p_s and p_t that eventually derive s and t, then p_s has higher priority than p_t iff s is predicted to precede t. Since Move only takes one argument s, replacing a Move prediction by the prediction of s trivially involves no such priority management. However, if movement is to a position to the left of s (as is standard for MGs), none of the lexical items contained within s can be scanned until the entire subtree moving out of s has been predicted and scanned.

If a prediction does not have the highest prior-

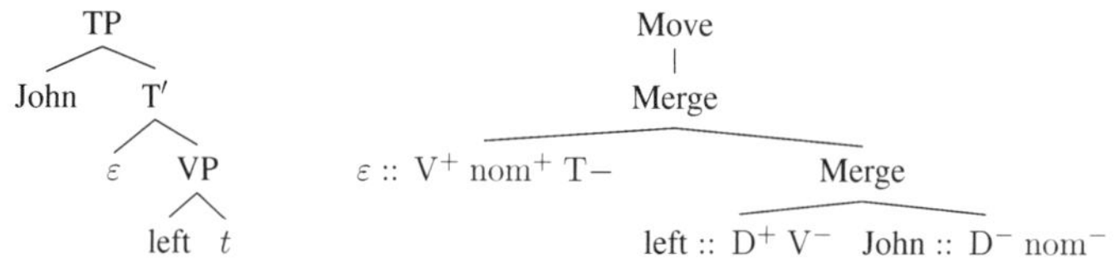

Figure 1: Minimalist phrase structure tree (left) and MG derivation tree (right) for *John left*

ity, it remains in the queue for a few steps before it is expanded into other predictions or discharged by scanning a word from the input string. The number of steps a prediction stays in the queue is called its *tenure*. With KGH's index notation, the tenure of each node is the difference between its indices. Given a parse, its *maximum tenure* **Max** is the smallest n such that the parser stored no prediction in its queue for more than n steps. KGH demonstrate that **Max** can be used to gauge how hard it is for humans to process certain structures. This amounts to equating processing difficulty with memory retention requirements. But as we show in the remainder of this paper, **Max** faces problems with relative clause constructions that were not considered by KGH.

3 Alternative Metrics

3.1 Three New Metrics

In an attempt to home in on the shortcomings of **Max**, we contrast it with a number of alternative metrics. Since the main advantage of **Max** is its simplicity, which makes it possible to quickly determine the processing predictions of a given syntactic analysis, the metrics we consider are also kept as simple as possible.

MaxLex the maximum tenure of all leaves in the derivation

Box the maximum number of nodes with tenure strictly greater than 2

BoxLex the maximum number of leaves with tenure strictly greater than 2

MaxLex is simply the restriction of **Max** to leaf nodes. **Box** and **BoxLex** provide a measure of how many items have to be stored in memory during the parse and hence incur some non-trivial amount of tenure. The threshold is set to 2 rather than 1 to exclude lexical items that are right siblings of another lexical item. In such a case, a single prediction is immediately followed by two consecutive scan steps, which could just as well be thought of as one scan step spanning two words. Nodes with tenure over 2 are highlighted by a box in our derivation trees, hence the name for these two metrics.

All four measures are also divided into two subtypes depending on whether unpronounced leaves (e.g. the empty T-head in Fig. 1) are taken into account — this is inspired by the exclusion of unpronounced material in the TAG-parser of Rambow and Joshi (1995). When reporting the values for the metrics, we thus give slashed values of the form m/n, where m is the value with unpronounced leaves and n the value without them.

3.2 Methodological Remarks

The following sections investigate the predictions of our difficulty metrics with respect to the embedding of sentential complements versus relative clauses, subject gaps versus object gaps in relative clauses, left embedding, and verb clusters. In order for this comparison to be meaningful, we have to make the same methodological assumptions as KGH.

First, the difficulty metric only has to account for overall sentence difficulty, it does not necessarily correlate with difficulty at a specific word. More importantly, though, all reported processing difficulties are assumed to be due to memory load. This is a very strong assumption. A plethora of alternative accounts are available in the literature. The contrast between subject gaps and object gaps alone has been explained by information-theoretic notions such as surprisal (Hale, 2003; Levy, 2013), the active filler strategy (Frazier and D'Arcais, 1989), or theta role assignment (Pritchett, 1992), to name but a few (see Lin (2006) and Wu (2009) for extensive surveys).

Even those accounts that attribute processing difficulty to memory requirements make ancillary assumptions that are not reflected by the simple memory model entertained here. Gibson's Dependency Locality Theory (1998), for instance, crucially relies on discourse reference as a means for determining how much of a memory burden is incurred by each word.

We take no stance as to whether these accounts are correct. Our primary interest is the feasibility of a memory-based evaluation metric for Stabler's top-down parser. Memory is more likely to play a role in the constructions we look at in the next two sections than in, say, attachment ambiguities or local syntactic coherence effects (Tabor et al., 2004). It may well turn out that memory is not involved at all, but for the purpose of comparing several memory-based metrics, they are the safest starting point.

4 Relative Clauses

4.1 Empirical Generalizations

Two major properties of relative clauses are firmly established in the literature (see Gibson (1998) and references therein).

- **SC/RC < RC/SC**
  A sentential complement containing a relative clause is easier to process than a relative clause containing a sentential complement.
- **SubjRC < ObjRC**
  A relative clause containing a subject gap is easier to parse than a relative clause containing an object gap.

These generalizations were obtained via self-paced reading experiments and ERP studies with minimal pairs such as (1) and (2), respectively.

(1) a. The fact [$_{\text{SC}}$ that the employee$_i$ [$_{\text{RC}}$ who the manager hired t_i] stole office supplies] worried the executive.

b. The executive$_i$ [$_{\text{RC}}$ who the fact [$_{\text{SC}}$ that the employee stole offices supplies] worried t_i] hired the manager.

(2) a. The reporter$_i$ [$_{\text{RC}}$ who t_i attacked the senator] admitted the error.

b. The reporter$_i$ [$_{\text{RC}}$ who the senator attacked t_i] admitted the error.

4.2 SC/RC and RC/SC

We first consider the contrast between relative clauses embedded inside a sentential complement (SC/RC) and relative clauses containing a sentential complement (SC/RC). Figures 2 and 3 on pages 5 and 6 show the augmented derivations for (1a) and (1b), respectively. For the sake of readability, we omit all features in our derivation trees and instead use standard X′ labels to indicate projection and dashed branches for movement.

Like KGH, we adopt a promotion analysis of relative clauses (Vergnaud, 1974; Kayne, 1994). That is to say, the head noun is selected by an empty determiner to form a DP, which starts out as an argument of the embedded verb and undergoes movement into the specifier of the relative clause (which is treated as an NP). The entire relative clause is then selected by the determiner that would usually select the head noun under the traditional, head-external analysis (Montague, 1970; Chomsky, 1977).[1]

In both derivations the maximum tenure obtains at two points in the matrix clause: I) the unpronounced T-head, and II) the Merge step that introduces the remainder of the VP. The parser must first build the entire subject before it can proceed scanning or expanding material to its right. Consequently, the tenure of these nodes increases with the size of the subject, and since both the SC/RC pattern and the RC/SC pattern necessarily involve large subjects, maximum tenure for both types of sentences is predicted to be relatively high. The parser shows a slightly lower **Max** value for SC/RC than for RC/SC — $32/32$ versus $33/33$.

Although this shows that strictly speaking **Max** is not incompatible with the generalization that SC/RC is easier to process than RC/SC, the difference is so small that even the presence of one more word in the SC/RC sentence could tip the balance towards RC/SC, which seems rather unlikely.

The contrast emerges more clearly with the other measures. **MaxLex** yields the values $32/9$ versus $33/17$, so it fares better than **Max** only if one ignores unpronounced leaves. This is expected since one of the nodes incurring the highest tenure value is the unpronounced T-head. The **Box** values are $14/11$ and $5/3$, and those of **BoxLex** are $12/9$ and $3/1$.

The box values fare better in this case because they are sensitive to the number of dependencies that cannot be discharged immediately. The way the MG parser traverses the tree, a sentential com-

[1]The promotion analysis was chosen to maintain consistency with KGH. But our observations hold for every analysis that involves some movement dependency between the gap and the specifier of the relative clause. This includes the more common head-external analyses mentioned above.

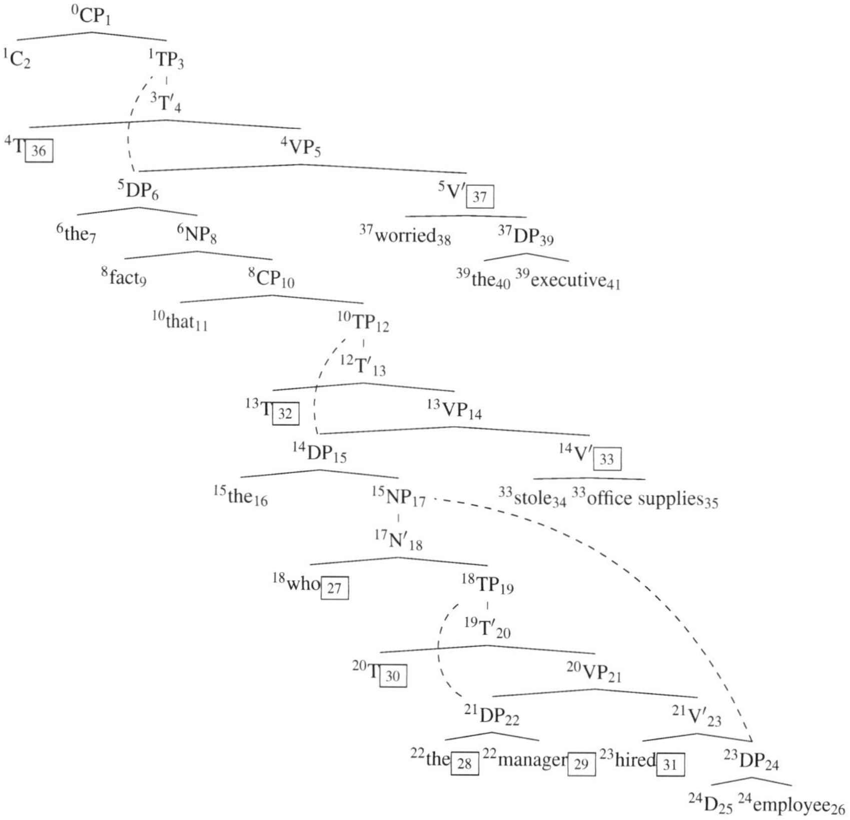

Figure 2: Sentential complement with embedded relative clause; **Max** $= 32/32$, **MaxLex** $= 32/9$, **Box** $= 9/6$, **BoxLex** $= 7/4$

plement in the subject position of a relative clause cannot be fully processed until the movement dependency within the relative clause has been taken care of. So even though the sentential complement is explored first, all its predicted elements must be kept in memory. A relative clause within the subject of a sentential complement, on the other hand, poses less of a challenge because the movement of its containing subject is so short that it only delays the processing of the T-head and V′.

4.3 Subject Gaps and Object Gaps

A stronger argument against **Max** is furnished by the preference for subject gaps over object gaps: maximum tenure is always the same for both constructions. Consider the derivations in Fig. 4 and 5 on pages 7 and 8. They have the same **Max** value because the maximum tenure once again obtains at the T-head of the matrix clause and the Merge node that expands the matrix VP. The tenure of these nodes is determined by the size of the subject, which contains the relative clause. But since the size of the subject is not affected by whether it is the subject or the object that is extracted from the relative clause, maximum tenure will never vary between these two constructions.

Once again the alternative metrics fare better than **Max**. **MaxLex** evaluates to $19/7$ and $19/9$. As before the tenure on the T-head causes **MaxLex** to behave like **Max** unless unpronounced words are ignored. If one does so, however, the maximum tenure value occurs on the relative pronoun *who* instead. Since *who* is the head of the relative clause, it is introduced early on during the structure building process, but it cannot be scanned until the parser reaches the element that moves into its specifier. Objects are more deeply embedded than subjects, and consequently it takes the parser less time to reach the subject than the object. As a result, *who* has greater tenure if the relative clause contains an object gap instead of a subject gap.

Box and **BoxLex** also predict the attested con-

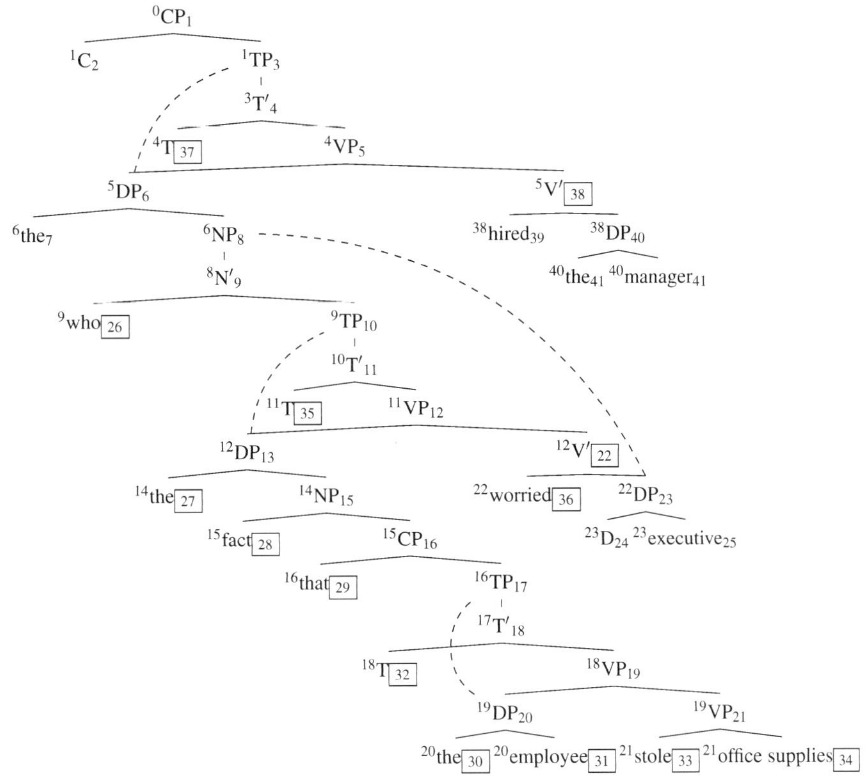

Figure 3: Relative clause containing a sentential complement; **Max** $= 33/33$, **MaxLex** $= 33/17$, **Box** $= 14/11$, **BoxLex** $= 12/9$

trast. **Box** produces the values $5/3$ and $7/5$, whereas **BoxLex** returns $3/1$ and $6/4$. Since subjects are introduced at a higher position than objects, movement of the subject causes fewer nodes to be delayed in their processing — the VP has not been fully expanded yet, so the nodes contained by it do not need to be stored in memory because the parser hasn't even predicted them at this point.

5 Further Observations

5.1 Verb Clusters in Dutch and German

KGH show that **Max** correctly predicts the attested difficulty differences between German and Dutch verb clusters (Bach et al., 1986). German verb clusters instantiate nested dependencies of the form DP_1 DP_2 $\cdots$ DP_n V_n $\cdots$ V_2 V_1. Dutch verb clusters, on the other hand, show crossing dependencies: DP_1 DP_2 $\cdots$ DP_n V_1 V_2 $\cdots$ V_n. Even though the latter not context-free and hence computationally more complex than the former, they are actually easier to process. Since KGH's account relies on the tenure of (pronounced) leaves, it also carries over to **MaxLex**.[2]

Box and **BoxLex**, however, do not make this prediction. In both Dutch and German every V_i has to be kept in memory before it can be scanned, so that a sentence with n verbs will have n boxes. According to **Box** and **BoxLex**, there should be no processing difference between German and Dutch. This can be partially fixed by summing the tenure of all boxed nodes so that overall memory load is at least partially taken into account, yielding the measures **SumBox** and **SumBoxLex**. But even those still make the wrong prediction for $n < 4$, that is to say, they establish the desired difference only after a point where both cluster types are already very hard to process.

[2]Strictly speaking KGH build their argument on the tenure of T, which **MaxLex** must ignore for the constructions investigated in this paper. However, tenure can be measured at V_1 instead, in which case Dutch clusters with three or more verbs have lower **MaxLex** values than the corresponding German clusters. Clusters consisting of only two verbs have the same **MaxLex** value in both languages. An anonymous reviewer points out that this is exactly the pattern found by Bach et al. (1986).

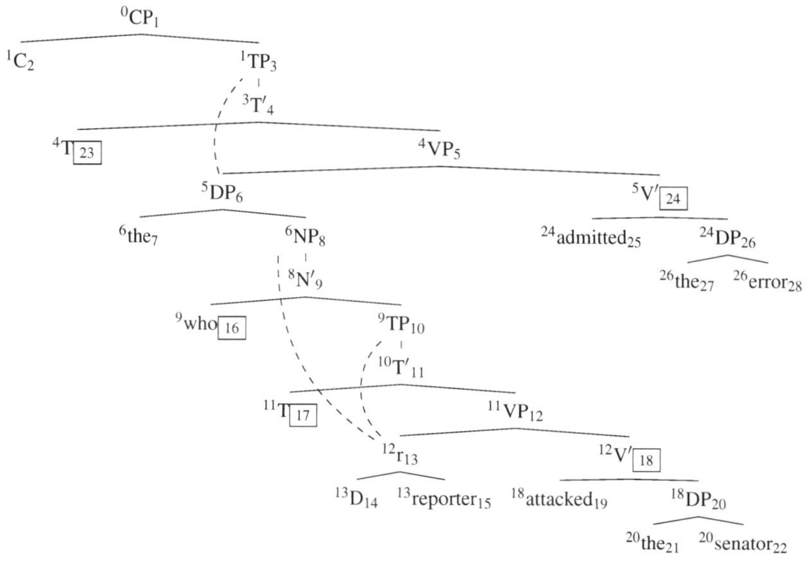

Figure 4: Relative clause with subject gap; **Max** $= 19/19$, **MaxLex** $= 19/7$, **Box** $= 5/3$, **BoxLex** $= 3/1$

5.2 Left Embedding

KGH note that if processing difficulty is determined by **Max**, then left embedding constructions such as English possessor nesting should lead to a sharp increase in parsing difficulty similar to center-embedding, which is not the case (Resnik, 1992).

(3) [[[Mike ['s uncle]] ['s cousin]] ['s roommate]] went to the store.

Box makes a similar prediction, whereas **MaxLex** and **BoxLex** do not (cf. Tab. 1 on page 1). Keep in mind that a left embedding construction c increases the tenure of the right sibling of c with every level of embedding. As long as c is not a lexical item, it will be ignored by **MaxLex** and **BoxLex**. Therefore possessor-embedding is predicted to be unproblematic, whereas a right-adjunction structure as in [$_{VP}$ [$_{VP}$ [$_{VP}$ left] quickly] yesterday] should increase the processing load. While we are not aware of any studies on this topic, such a split strikes us as highly unnatural.

5.3 Head-Final Relative Clauses

Preliminary work of ours suggests that almost none of the metrics covered in this paper work for languages where relative clauses precede their head nouns, such as Chinese, Japanese, and Korean. There is overwhelming evidence that these languages still show a preference for subject gaps over object gaps (Lin, 2006; Wu, 2009; Kwon et al., 2013). The syntactic structure of relative clauses in these languages is up to debate; but assuming that they involve rightward movement of the head noun into a specifier of the relative clause followed by remnant leftward movement of the TP into another specifier, most metrics derive a preference for object gaps (see the last two rows in Tab. 1). Only **Box** shows a small advantage for subject gaps.

6 Discussion and Future Work

Several metrics were compared in this paper that measure processing difficulty in terms of very different parameters: I) how long an item stays in memory (**Max**, **MaxLex**), II) how many items must be stored in memory (**Box**, **BoxLex**), and III) for what kind of material these criteria matter (±lexical, ±pronounced).

A quick glance at Tab. 1 reveals that no clear winner emerges. **Box** and **BoxLex** fail to capture the differences between Dutch and German verb clusters, whereas **Max** struggles with relative clause constructions and left embedding. **MaxLex** captures all these fact if only pronounced elements are taken into account, but makes the dubious prediction that right adjunction of a single word should be harder than left embedding or right adjunction of an adjunct that consists of at least two words. In addition, **MaxLex** fails to derive a subject gap preference for head-final relative clauses.

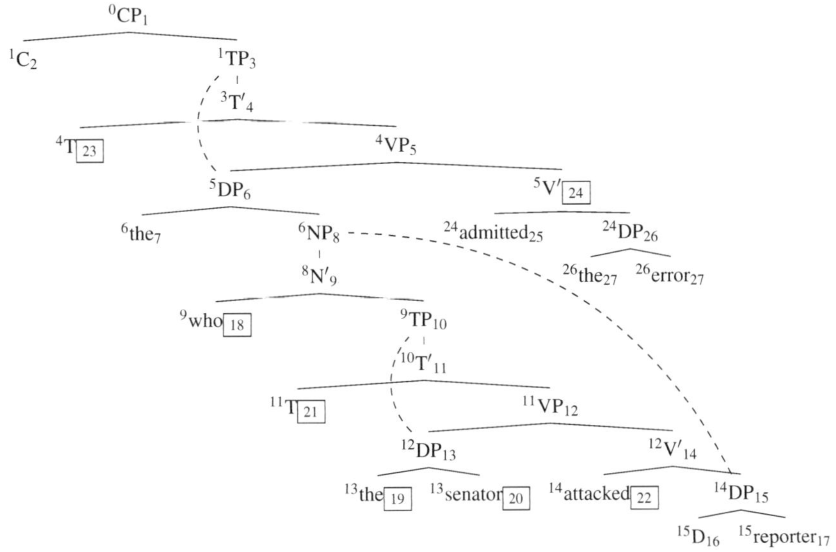

Figure 5: Relative clause with object gap; **Max** $= 19/19$, **MaxLex** $= 19/9$, **Box** $= 7/5$, **BoxLex** $= 6/4$

Phenomenon	Max	MaxLex	Box	BoxLex	SumBox	SumBoxLex
SC/RC	32/32	32/9	9/6	7/4	142/81	91/30
RC/SC	33/33	33/17	14/11	12/9	219/149	186/116
subject gap RC	19/19	19/7	5/3	3/1	57/32	32/7
object gap RC	19/19	19/9	7/5	6/4	78/49	59/30
1 possessor	7/7	7/2	2/1	1/0	14/7	7/0
2 possessors	11/11	11/2	3/2	1/0	27/16	11/0
3 possessors	15/15	15/2	4/3	1/0	46/31	15/0
1 right adjunct	7/7	7/3	3/2	2/1	17/10	10/3
2 right adjuncts	12/12	12/8	5/4	4/3	42/30	30/18
3 right adjuncts	15/15	15/12	7/6	6/5	58/43	43/28
crossing < nesting	yes	yes	no	no	partially	partially
head-final subj RC	20/20	20/11	5/4	4/3	66/39	46/19
head-final obj RC	20/20	20/10	6/4	3/1	63/38	35/10

Table 1: Overview of evaluation metrics

It is very likely that a more complicated metric could account for all these facts. But the appeal of **Max** and the alternatives investigated here is their simplicity. A simple metric is easier to study from a formal perspective. In an ideal world, the metric would turn out to correlate with a basic tree-geometric property of derivations so that the processing predictions of syntactic analyses can be determined at a glance without simulations or large-scale corpus work.

Two routes seems promising at this point. In order to rule out that the problem isn't with the metrics but rather the MG parser itself, the metrics should be tested with other parsing models. Those need not even be based on MGs, since the metrics measure aspects of memory management, which is an integral part of every parser.

Alternatively, we may look into how the metrics are applied. An anonymous reviewer points out that **Max** derives the preference for subject gaps if derivations that tie for **Max** are then compared with respect to the second-highest tenure value, which is $7/7$ for subject gaps and $10/9$ for object gaps. While this still leaves us with cases like left embedding where **Max** predicts a higher processing load than expected, it eliminates the problem of **Max** incorrectly equating two structures.

Acknowledgments

We are extremely grateful to the three anonymous reviewers. Their extensive comments not only brought about many improvements in the presentation and structure of the paper but also made us consider the wider implications of the work reported here.

References

David Adger. 2003. *Core Syntax: A Minimalist Approach.* Oxford University Press, Oxford.

Emmon Bach, Colin Brown, and William Marslen-Wilson. 1986. Crossed and nested dependencies in German and Dutch: A psycholinguistic study. *Language and Cognitive Processes*, 1:249–262.

Noam Chomsky. 1977. *Essays on Form and Interpretation.* New York, North Holland.

Noam Chomsky. 1995. *The Minimalist Program.* MIT Press, Cambridge, Mass.

Lyn Frazier and Flores D'Arcais. 1989. Filler driven parsing: A study of gap filling in Dutch. *Journal of Memory and Language*, 28:331–344.

Edward Gibson. 1998. Linguistic complexity: Locality of syntactic dependencies. *Cognition*, 68:1–76.

Thomas Graf. 2012. Locality and the complexity of minimalist derivation tree languages. In Philippe de Groot and Mark-Jan Nederhof, editors, *Formal Grammar 2010/2011*, volume 7395 of *Lecture Notes in Computer Science*, pages 208–227, Heidelberg. Springer.

John T. Hale. 2003. *Grammar, Uncertainty and Sentence Processing.* Ph.D. thesis, John Hopkins University.

Henk Harkema. 2001. A characterization of minimalist languages. In Philippe de Groote, Glyn Morrill, and Christian Retoré, editors, *Logical Aspects of Computational Linguistics (LACL'01)*, volume 2099 of *Lecture Notes in Artificial Intelligence*, pages 193–211. Springer, Berlin.

Aravind Joshi. 1985. Tree-adjoining grammars: How much context sensitivity is required to provide reasonable structural descriptions? In David Dowty, Lauri Karttunen, and Arnold Zwicky, editors, *Natural Language Parsing*, pages 206–250. Cambridge University Press, Cambridge.

Richard S. Kayne. 1994. *The Antisymmetry of Syntax.* MIT Press, Cambridge, Mass.

Gregory M. Kobele, Christian Retoré, and Sylvain Salvati. 2007. An automata-theoretic approach to minimalism. In James Rogers and Stephan Kepser, editors, *Model Theoretic Syntax at 10*, pages 71–80.

Gregory M. Kobele, Sabrina Gerth, and John T. Hale. 2012. Memory resource allocation in top-down minimalist parsing. In *Proceedings of Formal Grammar 2012.*

Nayoung Kwon, Robert Kluender, Marta Kutas, and Maria Polinsky. 2013. Subject/object processing asymmetries in korean relative clauses: Evidence from ERP data. *Language*, 89:537–585.

Roger Levy. 2013. Memory and surprisal in human sentence comprehension. In Roger P. G. van Gompel, editor, *Sentence Processing*, pages 78–114. Psychology Press, Hove.

Chien-Jer Charles Lin. 2006. *Grammar and Parsing: A Typological Investigation of Relative-Clause Processing.* Ph.D. thesis, University of Arizona.

Jens Michaelis. 2001. Transforming linear context-free rewriting systems into minimalist grammars. *Lecture Notes in Artificial Intelligence*, 2099:228–244.

Richard Montague. 1970. English as a formal language. In Bruno Visentini and et al., editors, *Linguaggi nella Societ e nella Tecnica*, pages 189–224. Edizioni di Comunit, Milan.

Bradley L. Pritchett. 1992. *Grammatical Competence and Parsing Performance.* University of Chicago Press, Chicago.

Owen Rambow and Aravind Joshi. 1995. A processing model for free word order languages. Technical Report IRCS-95-13, University of Pennsylvania.

Philip Resnik. 1992. Left-corner parsing and psychological plausibility. In *Proceedings of COLING-92*, pages 191–197.

Edward P. Stabler. 1997. Derivational minimalism. In Christian Retoré, editor, *Logical Aspects of Computational Linguistics*, volume 1328 of *Lecture Notes in Computer Science*, pages 68–95. Springer, Berlin.

Edward P. Stabler. 2011a. Computational perspectives on minimalism. In Cedric Boeckx, editor, *Oxford Handbook of Linguistic Minimalism*, pages 617–643. Oxford University Press, Oxford.

Edward P. Stabler. 2011b. Top-down recognizers for MCFGs and MGs. In *Proceedings of the 2011 Workshop on Cognitive Modeling and Computational Linguistics.* to appear.

Edward P. Stabler. 2012. Bayesian, minimalist, incremental syntactic analysis. *Topics in Cognitive Science*, 5:611–633.

Whitney Tabor, Bruno Galantucci, and Daniel Richardson. 2004. Effects of merely local syntactic coherence on sentence processing. *Journal of Memory and Language*, 50:355–370.

Jean-Roger Vergnaud. 1974. *French Relative Clauses.* Ph.D. thesis, MIT.

Fuyun Wu. 2009. *Factors Affecting Relative Clause Processing in Mandarin.* Ph.D. thesis, University of Southern California.

Learning Verb Classes in an Incremental Model

Libby Barak, Afsaneh Fazly, and **Suzanne Stevenson**
Department of Computer Science
University of Toronto
Toronto, Canada
{libbyb,afsaneh,suzanne}@cs.toronto.edu

Abstract

The ability of children to generalize over the linguistic input they receive is key to acquiring productive knowledge of verbs. Such generalizations help children extend their learned knowledge of constructions to a novel verb, and use it appropriately in syntactic patterns previously unobserved for that verb—a key factor in language productivity. Computational models can help shed light on the gradual development of more abstract knowledge during verb acquisition. We present an incremental Bayesian model that simultaneously and incrementally learns argument structure constructions and verb classes given naturalistic language input. We show how the distributional properties in the input language influence the formation of generalizations over the constructions and classes.

1 Introduction

Usage-based accounts of language learning note that young children rely on verb-specific knowledge to produce their early utterances (e.g., Tomasello, 2003). However, evidence suggests that even young children can generalize their verb knowledge to novel verbs and syntactic frames (e.g., Fisher, 2002), and that the abstract knowledge gradually strengthens over time (e.g., Tomasello and Abbot-Smith, 2002). One area of verb usage where more sophisticated abstraction appears necessary for fully adult productivity in language is the knowledge of verb alternations. A verb alternation is a pairing of constructions shared by a number of verbs, in which the two constructions express related argument structures (Levin, 1993): e.g., the dative alternation involves the related forms of the prepositional dative (PD; *X gave Y to Z*) and the double-object dative (DO; *X gave Z Y*). Such alternations enable language users to readily adapt new and low frequency verbs to appropriate constructions of the language by generalizing the observed use of one such form to the other.[1]

For example, Conwell and Demuth (2007) show that 3-year-old children understand that a novel verb observed only in the DO dative (*John gorped Heather the book*) can also be used in the PD form (*John gorped the book to Heather*), though the children can only generalize such knowledge under certain experimental conditions. Wonnacott et al. (2008) demonstrate the proficiency of adults in making such generalizations within an artificial language learning scenario, which enables the researchers to explore the distributional properties of the linguistic input that facilitate the acquisition of such generalizations. The results suggest that the overall frequency of the syntactic patterns as well as the distribution of verbs across the patterns play a facilitatory role in the formation of abstract verb knowledge (in the form of verb alternations) in adult language learners.

In this work, we propose a computational model that extends an existing Bayesian model of verb argument structure acquisition (Alishahi and Stevenson, 2008)[AS08] to support the learning of verb classes over the acquired constructions. Our model is novel in its approach to verb class formation, because it clusters tokens of a verb that reflect the distribution of the verb over the learned constructions each time the verb is used in an input. That is, the model forms verb classes by clustering verb tokens that reflect the evolving usages of the verbs in various constructions.

We use this new model to analyze the role of the classes and the distributional properties of the input in learning abstract verb knowledge, given

[1]The *generalization of an alternation* refers to a speaker using one variant of an alternation for a verb (e.g., PD) having only observed the verb in the other variant (e.g., DO).

Proceedings of the 2014 ACL Workshop on Cognitive Modeling and Computational Linguistics, pages 37–45,
Baltimore, Maryland USA, June 26 2014.

naturalistic input that contains many verbs and many constructions. The model can form higher-level generalizations such as learning verb alternations, which is not possible with the AS08 model (cf. the findings of Parisien and Stevenson, 2010). Moreover, because our model gradually forms its representations of constructions and classes over time (in contrast to other Bayesian models, such as Parisien and Stevenson, 2010; Perfors et al., 2010), it is possible to analyze the monotonically-growing representations and show their compatibility with the developmental patterns seen in children (Conwell and Demuth, 2007). We also replicate some of the observations of Wonnacott et al. (2008) on the role of distributional properties of the language in influencing the degree of generalization over an alternation.

2 Related Work

To explore the properties of learning mechanisms that are capable of mimicking child and adult psycholinguistic observations, a number of cognitive modeling studies have focused on learning abstract verb knowledge from individual verb usages (e.g., Alishahi and Stevenson, 2008; Perfors et al., 2010; Parisien and Stevenson, 2010). Here we focus on such computational models that enable the sort of higher-level generalization that people do across verb alternations, unlike the AS08 model.

The hierarchical Bayesian models of Perfors et al. (2010) and Parisien and Stevenson (2010) focus on learning this kind of higher-level generalization. The model of Perfors et al. (2010) learns verb alternations, i.e., pairs of syntactic patterns shared by certain groups of verbs. By incorporating this sort of abstract knowledge into their model, Perfors et al. are able to simulate the ability of adults to generalize across verb alternations (as in Wonnacott et al., 2008). That is, Perfors et al. predict the ability of a novel verb to occur in a syntactic structure after exposure to it in the alternative pattern of that alternation. However, this model is trained on data that contains only a limited number of verbs and syntactic patterns unlike naturalistic Child-directed Speech (CDS) and moreover incorporates built-in information about verb constructions.

The hierarchical Dirichlet model of Parisien and Stevenson (2010) addresses these limitations by working with natural child-directed speech (CDS) data. Moreover, the model of Parisien and Stevenson simultaneously learns constructions as in AS08 and verb classes based on verb alternation behaviour, showing that the latter level of abstraction is necessary to support effective learning of verb alternations. Still, the models of both Parisien and Stevenson and Perfors et al. can only be utilized as a batch process and hence are limited in the analysis of developmental trajectories. Although it is possible to simulate development by training such models on increasing portions of input, such an approach does not ensure that the representations given $n + i$ inputs can be developed from the representation given n inputs.

In this paper, we propose a significant extension to the model of AS08, by adding an extra level of abstraction that incrementally learns verb classes by drawing on the distribution of verbs over the learned constructions. The new model combines the advantages of having a monotonic clustering model that enables the analysis of developing clusters, with the simultaneous learning of constructions and verb classes.

3 The Computational Model

As mentioned above, our model is an extension of the model of AS08 in which we add a level of learned abstract knowledge about verbs. Specifically, our model uses a Bayesian clustering process to learn clusters of verb usages that occur in similar argument structure constructions, as in the original model of AS08. To this, we add another level of abstraction that learns clusters of verbs that exhibit similar distributional patterns of occurrence across the learned constructions—that is, classes of verbs that occur in similar *sets of* constructions, and in similar proportions. To distinguish between the clusters of the two levels of abstraction in our new model, we refer to the clusters of verb usages as constructions, and to the groupings of verbs given their distribution over those constructions as verb classes.

3.1 Overview of the Model

The model learns from a sequence of *frames*, where each frame is a collection of *features* representing what the learner might extract from an utterance s/he has heard. Similarly to previous computational studies (e.g., Parisien and Stevenson, 2010), here we focus on syntactic features since our goal is to understand the acquisition of acceptable syntactic structures of verbs indepen-

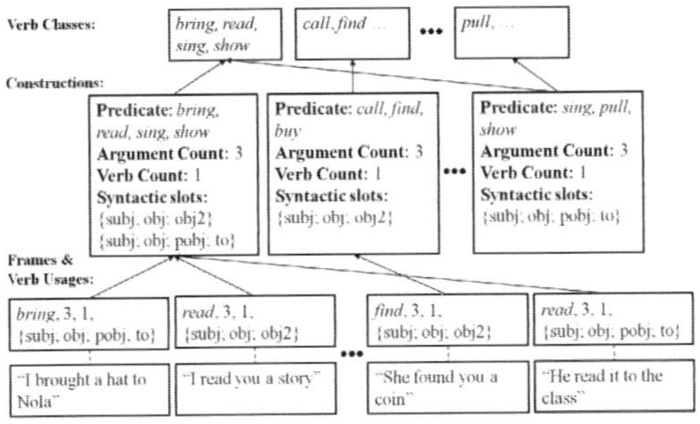

Figure 1: A visual representation of the two levels of abstraction in the model, with sample verb usages input (and extracted input frames), constructions, and classes.

dently of their meaning, as in some relevant psycholinguistic (Wonnacott et al., 2008) and computational studies (Parisien and Stevenson, 2010). We focus particularly on properties such as *syntactic slots* and *argument count*. (These features, as in Parisien and Stevenson (2010), provide a more flexible and generalizable representation of a syntactic structure than the syntactic pattern string used by AS08.) See the bottom rows of boxes in Figure 1 for sample input verb usages with their extracted frames.

The model incrementally clusters the extracted input frames into *constructions* that reflect probabilistic associations of the features across similar verb usages; see the middle level of Figure 1. Each learned cluster is a probabilistic (and possibly noisy) representation of an argument structure construction: e.g., a cluster containing frames corresponding to usages such as *I eat apples*, *She took the ball*, and *He got a book*, etc., represents a Transitive Action construction.[2] Such constructions allow for some degree of generalization over the observed input; e.g., when seeing a novel verb in a Transitive utterance, the model predicts the similarity of this verb to other Action verbs appearing in that pattern (Alishahi and Stevenson, 2008).

Grouping of verb usages into constructions may not be sufficient for making higher-level generalizations across verb alternations. Knowledge of alternations is only captured indirectly in constructions (because usages of the same verb can occur in multiple clusters). Following Parisien and Stevenson (2010), we hypothesize that true generalization behaviour requires explicit knowledge that verbs have commonalities in their patterns of occurrence *across* constructions; this is the basis for verb classes (Levin, 1993; Merlo and Stevenson, 2000; Schulte im Walde and Brew, 2002).

[2]Because the associations are probabilistic, a linguistic construction may be represented by more than one cluster.

To capture this, our model learns groupings of verbs that have similar distributions across the learned constructions. These groupings form verb classes that provide a higher-level of abstraction over the input; see the top level in Figure 1. Consider the dative alternation: the classes capture the fact that some verbs may occur only in prepositional dative (PD) forms, such as *sing*, while others occur only in double object (DO) forms (*call*), while still others *alternate* – i.e., they occur in both (*bring*).

Our model simultaneously learns both of these types of knowledge: constructions are clusters of verb usages, and classes are clusters of verb distributions over those constructions. Importantly, it does so incrementally, which allows us to examine the developmental trajectory of acquiring alternations such as the dative as the learned clusters grow over time. Moreover, both types of clustering are monotonic, i.e., we do not re-structure the groupings that our model learns. However, the model in both levels is clustering *verb tokens* – i.e., the features corresponding to the verb at that time in the input, its usage or its current distribution – so that the same verb type may be added to various clusters at different stages in the training.

3.2 Learning Constructions of Verb Usages

The model of AS08 groups input frames into clusters on the basis of the overall similarity in the values of their features. Importantly, the model learns these clusters incrementally in response to the input; the number and type of clusters is not predetermined. The model considers the creation of a new cluster for a given frame if the frame is not sufficiently similar to any of the existing clusters. Formally, the model finds the best cluster for a given input frame F as in:

$$\text{BestCluster}(F) = \underset{k \in Clusters}{\text{argmax}} \; P(k|F) \quad (1)$$

where k ranges over all existing clusters and a new one. Using Bayes rule:

$$P(k|F) = \frac{P(k)P(F|k)}{P(F)} \propto P(k)P(F|k) \quad (2)$$

The prior probability of a cluster $P(k)$ is estimated as the proportion of frames that are in k out of all observed input frames, thus assigning a higher prior more frequent constructions. The likelihood $P(F|k)$ is estimated based on the match of feature values in F and in the frames of k (assuming independence of the features):

$$P(F|k) = \prod_{i \in Features} P_i(j|k) \quad (3)$$

where j is the value of the ith feature of F, and $P_i(j|k)$ is calculated using a smoothed version of:

$$P_i(j|k) = \frac{\text{count}_i(j,k)}{n_k} \quad (4)$$

where $\text{count}_i(j,k)$ is the number of times feature i has the value j in cluster k, and n_k is the number of frames in k. We compare the slot features as sets to capture similarities in overlapping syntactic slots rather than enforcing an exact match. The model uses the Jaccard similarity score to measure the degree of overlap between two feature sets, instead of the direct count of occurrence in Eqn. (4):

$$\text{sim\_score}(S_1, S_2) = \frac{|S_1 \cap S_2|}{|S_1 \cup S_2|} \quad (5)$$

where S_1 and S_2 in our experiments here are the sets of syntactic slot features.

3.3 Learning Verb Classes

Our new model extends the construction-formation model of AS08 by grouping verbs into classes on the basis of their distribution across the learned constructions. That is, verbs that have statistically-similar patterns of occurrence across the learned constructions will be considered as forming a verb class. For example, in Figure 1 we see that *bring* and *read* may be put into the same class because they both occur in a similar relative frequency across the DO and PD constructions (the leftmost and rightmost constructions in the figure).

We use the same incremental Bayesian clustering algorithm for learning the verb classes as for learning constructions. At the class level, the feature used for determining similarity of items in clustering is the distribution of each verb across the learned constructions. As for constructions, the model learns the verb classes incrementally; the number and type is not predetermined. Moreover, just as constructions are gradually formed from successively processing a particular verb usage at each input step, the model forms verb classes from a sequence of snapshots of the input verb's distribution over the constructions at each input step. This means that our model is forming classes of verb tokens rather than types; if a verb's behaviour changes over the duration of the input, subsequent tokens (the distributions over constructions at later points in time) may be clustered into a different class (or classes) than earlier tokens, even though prior decisions cannot be undone.

Formally, after clustering the input frame at time t into a construction, as explained above, the model extracts the current distribution d_{v_t} of its head verb v over the learned constructions; this is estimated as a smoothed version of v's relative frequency in each construction:

$$P(k|v) = \frac{\text{count}(v,k)}{n_v} \quad (6)$$

where $\text{count}(v,k)$ is the number of times that inputs with verb v have been clustered into construction k, and n_v is the number of times v has occurred in the input thus far.

To cluster this snapshot of the verb's distribution, d_{v_t}, it is compared to the distributions encoded by the model's classes. The distribution d_c of an existing class c is the weighted average of the distributions of its member verb tokens:

$$d_c = \frac{1}{|c|} \sum_{v \in c} \text{count}(v,c) \times d_v \quad (7)$$

where $|c|$ is the size of class c, $\text{count}(v,c)$ is the number of occurrences of v that have been assigned to c, and d_v is the distribution of the verb v given by the tokens of v (the "snapshots" of distributions of v assigned to class c). That is, d_v in c is an average of the distributions of all d_{v_t} for verb v that have been clustered into c.

The model finds the best class for a given verb distribution d_{v_t} based on its similarity to the distributions of all existing classes and a new one:

$$\text{BestClass}(d_{v_t}) = \underset{c \in Classes}{\text{argmax}} \; (1 - D_{\text{JS}}(d_c \| d_{v_t})) \quad (8)$$

where c ranges over all existing classes as well as a new class that is represented as a uniform distribution over the existing constructions. Jensen–Shannon divergence, D_{JS}, is a popular method for measuring the distance between two distributions: It is based on the KL–divergence, but it is symmetric and has a finite value between 0 and 1:

$$D_{\text{JS}}(p\|q) = \frac{1}{2} D_{\text{KL}}(p \| \frac{1}{2}(p+q)) + \frac{1}{2} D_{\text{KL}}(q \| \frac{1}{2}(p+q)) \quad (9)$$

	non-ALT		ALT	
	DO-only	PD-only	DO	PD
Number of verbs	12	5	6	
Relative frequency	14%	2%	2%	1%

Table 1: Number of non-alternating (non-ALT) and alternating (ALT) verbs in our lexicon, as well as the relative frequency of each construction in our generated input corpora.

4 Experimental Setup

4.1 Generation of the Input Corpora

We follow the input generation method of AS08 to create naturalistic corpora that are based on the distributional properties of verbs over various constructions, as observed in child-directed speech (CDS). Our *input-generation lexicon* contains 71 verbs drawn from AS08 (11 action verbs) and Barak et al. (2013) (31 verbs of varying syntactic patterns), plus an additional 40 of the most frequent verbs in CDS, in order to have a range of verbs that occur with the PD and DO constructions. Table 4.1 shows the number of verbs that appear in the DO or PD construction only (non-alternating), as well as those that alternate across the two. (The table also gives the relative frequency of each dative construction in our generated input corpora.) Each verb lexical entry includes its overall frequency, and its relative frequency with each of a number of observed syntactic constructions. The frequencies are extracted from a manual annotation of a sample of 100 child-directed utterances per verb from a collection of eight corpora from CHILDES (MacWhinney, 2000).[3] An input corpus is generated by iteratively selecting a random verb and a syntactic construction based on their frequencies according to the lexicon, so that all input corpora used in our simulations have the distributional properties observed in CDS, but show some variation in precise make-up and ordering of verb usages. The generated input consists of *frames* (a set of features) that correspond to verb usages in CDS.

4.2 Simulations

Because the generation of the input data is probabilistic, we conduct 100 simulations for each experiment (each using a different input corpus) to avoid any dependency on specific idiosyncratic properties of a single generated corpus. For each simulation, we train our model on an automatically-generated corpus of $15,000$ frames, from which the model learns constructions and verb classes. At specified points in the input, we present the model with usages of a novel verb in a DO and/or PD frame, and then test the model's generalization ability by predicting DO and PD frames given that verb. Since we are interested in the relative likelihoods of the two frames, we report the difference between the log-likelihood of the DO frame and the log-likelihood of the PD frame, i.e., $\text{log-likelihood}(\text{DO}) - \text{log-likelihood}(\text{PD})$.

Specifically, we form a partial frame F_{test} (containing all usage features except for the verb) that reflects either the PD or the DO syntax, and assess the probability $P(F_{\text{test}}|v)$ for each of these, as in:

$$P(F_{\text{test}}|v) = \sum_{k \in Constructions} P(F_{\text{test}}|k)P(k|v) \quad (10)$$

where $P(F_{\text{test}}|k)$ is calculated as in Eqn. (3).

We can calculate $P(k|v)$ in two different ways: using only the knowledge in the constructions of the model, and using the knowledge that takes into account the verb classes over the constructions. For model predictions based on the construction level only, we calculate $P(k|v)$ as in Eqn. (6), which is the smoothed relative frequency of the verb v over construction k.

Predictions using knowledge of the verb classes will instead determine $P(k|v)$ drawing on the fit of verb v to the various classes (specifically, the similarity of v's distribution over constructions to the distribution encoded in each class), and the likelihood of each construction k for each class c (specifically, the likelihood of k given the distribution over constructions encoded in c), as in:

$$P(k|v) \approx \sum_{c \in Classes} P(k|c)P(c|v) \quad (11)$$

where $P(k|c)$ is the probability of construction k given class c's distribution over constructions (d_c); and $P(c|v)$ is the probability of c given verb v's distribution d_v over the constructions (using Jensen-Shannon divergence as in Eqn. (9)).

Due to the different number of clusters in each of the construction and class layers of the model, the likelihoods computed for each will differ in the range of values. For this reason, specific values cannot be directly compared across the layers of the model, rather we must analyze the general trends of the construction-only and class-based results.

[3] Brown (1973); Suppes (1974); Kuczaj (1977); Bloom et al. (1974); Sachs (1983); Lieven et al. (2009).

5 Evaluation

In this section we examine whether and how our model generalizes across the two variants of the dative alternation, the double-object dative (DO) and the prepositional dative (PD). To do so, we measure the tendency of the model to produce a novel verb observed in one dative frame in that same frame, or in the other dative frame (unobserved for that verb). Our goal is to understand the impact of the learned constructions and classes on this generalization behaviour. Following Parisien and Stevenson (2010), we examine three input conditions in which the novel verb occurs: (i) twice with the DO syntax (non-alternating); (ii) twice with the PD syntax (non-alternating); or (iii) once each with DO and PD syntax (alternating).[4] We then ask the model to predict the likelihood of producing each dative frame with that verb. Our focus here is on comparing the generalization abilities of the two levels of abstract knowledge in our model: the constructions versus the verb classes.

As a reminder, we use the dative alternation as one example for considering this kind of higher-level generalization behaviour observed in adults and to a lesser extent in children. Moreover, we perform the analysis in the context of naturalistic input that contains many verbs (those that appear in the dative and those that do not), and a variety of constructions , to provide a realistic setting for the task. Our settings differ from the psycholinguistic studies in the variability of constructions compared with the artificial language used by Wonnacott et al., and in focusing only on the syntactic properties unlike Conwell and Demuth. However, we follow the settings of these studies in analyzing the syntactic properties of a generated utterance given minimal exposure to a novel verb. Therefore, we aim to replicate their general observations by showing that (i) children are limited in their ability to generalize across verb alternations compared with adults, and (ii) the frequency of a construction has a positive correlation with the generalization rate of the construction.

5.1 Generalization of Learned Knowledge

We examine the generalization patterns of our model when presented with a novel verb in DO/PD forms after being trained on $15,000$ inputs, which we compare to the performance of adults in such language tasks. We first consider the case where the model predictions are based solely on the knowledge of constructions. Here we expect the predictions to correspond to the syntactic properties of the two inputs observed for the novel verb, with limited generalization. That is, we expect a non-alternating verb to be much more likely in the observed dative frame, and an alternating verb to be equally likely in both frames. The left hand side of Figure 2 presents the differences in log-likelihoods of the predicted DO and PD frames for the novel verb using the construction-based probabilities. The results confirm our expectation that the knowledge of constructions can support only limited generalization *across* the variants of an alternation. For the non-alternating conditions, the observed frame is highly favoured, and for the Alternating test scenario, the DO and PD frames have nearly equal likelihoods.

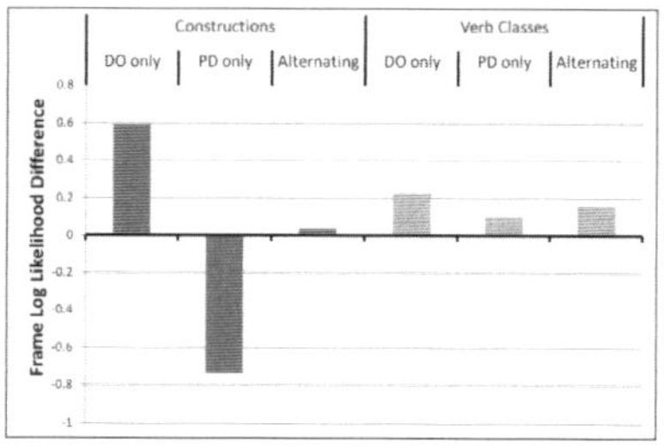

Figure 2: The difference between the log-likelihood values of the DO and PD frames, given each of the three input conditions: DO only, PD only, and Alternating. Values above zero denote a higher likelihood for the DO frame, and values below zero denote a higher likelihood for the PD frame.

We next turn to using the knowledge of verb classes, which we expect to enable generalizations that correspond to verb alternation behaviour — that is, we expect the model predictions here to reflect the knowledge that verbs that occur in one form of the alternation also often occur in the other form of the alternation. This is possible because the classes in the model encode the distributional patterns of verbs across constructions. In the absence of other factors, we would expect the Alternating condition to again show near equal likelihoods for the two frames, and the two non-alternating conditions to show a slight preference for the observed frame (rather than the strong preference seen in the construction-based predictions), because the unobserved frame is also likely due to the knowledge here of the alternation.

The right hand side of Figure 2 presents the

[4]For the alternating condition, half the simulations have DO first, and half have PD first.

difference in the log-likelihoods of the DO and PD frames when using the knowledge encoded in the verb classes. The results are not directly in line with the simple prediction above: The non-alternating (DO-only and PD-only) conditions show a weak preference (as expected) for one frame over another, but both favour the DO frame, as does the Alternating condition. That is, the PD-only and Alternating conditions show a preference for the DO frame that does not follow simply from the knowledge of alternations.

The DO preference in the PD-only and Alternating conditions arises due to distributional factors in the input, related to the frequencies of the constructions reported in Table 1. First, the DO frame is overall much more likely than the PD frame, causing generalization in the PD-only and Alternating conditions to lean more to that frame. Second, fully $1/3$ of the uses of the PD frame in the corpus are with verbs that alternate (i.e., 1% of the corpus are PD frames of alternating PD-DO verbs, out of a total of 3% of the corpus being PD frames), while only $1/8$ of the uses of the DO frame are with alternating rather than non-alternating verbs. Recall that our classes encode the distribution (roughly relative frequency) of the verbs in the class occurring across the different constructions. This means that in our class-based predictions, greater weight will be given to constructions with DO when observing a PD frame than to constructions with PD when observing a DO frame. These results underline the importance of using naturalistic input and considering the impact of various distributional factors on generalization of verb knowledge.

In contrast to the construction-based results, our class-based results conform with the experimental findings of Wonnacott et al. (2008), who show that adult (artificial) language learners robustly generalize a newly-learned verb observed in a single syntactic form by producing it in the alternating syntactic form under certain language conditions. Moreover, we show similar distributional effects to theirs – the overall frequency of the syntactic patterns, as well as the distribution of verbs across those patterns – in the level of preference for one form over another, within the context of our naturalistic data with multiple verbs, constructions, and alternations. These results show that the verb classes in the model are able to capture useful abstract knowledge that is key to understanding the human ability to make high-level generalizations across verb alternations.

5.2 Development of Generalizations

Next, we present the results of our model evaluated throughout the course of training in order to understand the developmental pattern of generalization. We perform the same construction-based or class-based prediction tasks (the likelihoods of a DO and PD frame), following the same input conditions (a novel verb with two DO frames, two PD frames, or one of each) at given points during the $15,000$ inputs. As above, we present the difference in the log-likelihood values of the DO and the PD frames in order to focus on the relative likelihoods of the two frames within each condition of construction-based or class-based predictions.

Figure 3(a) presents the results for the DO-only test scenario. As in Section 5.1, for both construction-based and class-based predictions there is a higher likelihood for the DO frame throughout the course of training. In contrast, the incremental results for the PD-only test scenario, in Figure 3(b), display a developing level of generalization throughout the training stage for the class-based predictions. While the construction-based predictions reflect a much higher likelihood for the PD frame, the results from the verb classes are in favor of the PD frame only initially; after training on 5000 input frames, the likelihood of the DO frame becomes higher for this test scenario. These results indicate that using construction knowledge alone does not enable generalization from the PD frame to the DO frame; in contrast, the verb class knowledge enables the gradual acquisition of generalization ability over the course of training.

Finally, Figure 3(c) presents the results for the Alternating test scenario for the two types of predictions. As in Section 5.1, both construction-based and class-based predictions have a small preference for the DO frame. In the construction-based predictions, this preference lessens over time to where the likelihoods for DO and PD are almost equal, while the class-based predictions stay relatively constant in their preference for the DO frame. In some ways the construction-based predictions are more expected in response to an apparently alternating verb; however, the class-based predictions show a higher degree of generalization, responding to the higher frequency of the

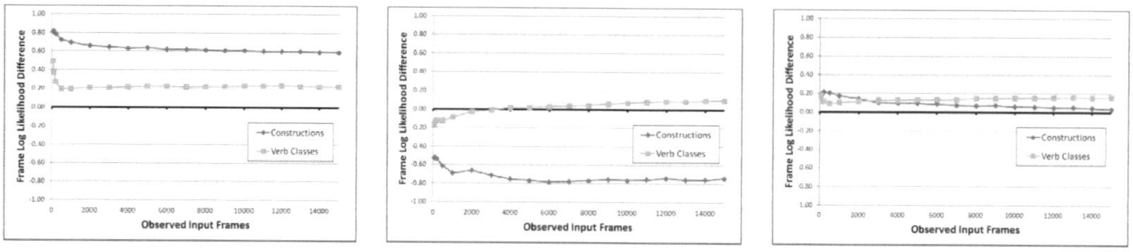

(a) DO only (b) PD only (c) Alternating

Figure 3: Difference of log-likelihood values of the DO and PD frames over the course of training for the constructions and the verb classes for each of the 3 test scenarios. Values above zero denote a higher likelihood for the DO frame, and values below zero denote a higher likelihood for the PD frame.

DO frame and the higher association of PD frames with DO alternates. These results again emphasize the importance of further exploring the role of distributional factors on generalization of verb knowledge in children.

The developmental results presented here are in line with the suggestions of Tomasello (2003) that the productions of younger children follow observed patterns in the input, and only later reflect robust generalizations of their knowledge across verbs. Conwell and Demuth (2007) for example, found evidence of generalization across verb alternations in 3-year-old children, but their production of unobserved forms for a novel verb was very sensitive to the precise context of the experiment and the distributional patterns across the novel verbs. In accord with these observations, the developmental trajectories in our model show that our class-based predictions increase in their degree of generalization over time, and are sensitive to various distributional factors in the input, such as the overall expectation for a frame and the expectation that a verb will alternate.

6 Discussion

We present a novel computational model that probabilistically learns two levels of abstractions over individual verb usages: constructions that are clusters of similar verb usages, and classes of verbs with similar distributional behaviour across the constructions. Specifically, we extend the model of AS08 by incrementally learning token-based verb classes that generalize over the construction knowledge level. In contrast to the models of Parisien and Stevenson and Perfors et al., our model is incremental, and hence enables the analysis of the monotonically developing classes to show the relation to the development of generalization ability in human learners.

We analyze how generalization is supported by each level of learning in our model: constructions and verb classes. Our results confirm (cf. Parisien and Stevenson, 2010) that a higher-level knowledge of the verb classes is required to replicate the observed patterns of generalization, such as producing a novel verb *gorp* in the in the prepositional dative pattern after hearing it in the double object dative pattern. In addition, our analysis of the incrementally developing verb classes shows that the generalization knowledge gradually emerges over time, similar to what is observed in children.

The flexibility of input representation of our model enables us to further explore the properties of the input in learning abstract knowledge, following psycholinguistic studies. Our results replicate the findings of Wonnacott et al. on the role of the distributional properties over the alternating syntactic forms, but in naturalistic settings of many constructions. In future, we plan to extend this analysis by manipulating the distributions of our input data to replicate the exact settings of the artificial language used by Wonnacott et al.. Moreover, in this study, we followed the settings of previous computational and psycholinguistic studies that focused on the syntactic properties of the input (Perfors et al., 2010; Parisien and Stevenson, 2010; Wonnacott et al., 2008; Conwell and Demuth, 2007). However, we can further our analysis by incorporating semantic features in the input to study syntactic bootstrapping effects (Scott and Fisher, 2009) as well as the role of semantic properties in constraining the generalizations across the alternating forms.

Acknowledgments

The authors would like to thank Afra Alishahi for providing us with the code and data for her model, and to Chris Parisien for sharing his data with us.

References

Afra Alishahi and Suzanne Stevenson. 2008. A computational model of early argument structure acquisition. *Cognitive Science*, 32(5):789–834.

Libby Barak, Afsaneh Fazly, and Suzanne Stevenson. 2013. Acquisition of desires before beliefs: A computational investigation. In *Proceedings of CoNLL-2013*.

Lois Bloom, Lois Hood, and Patsy Lightbown. 1974. Imitation in language development: If, when, and why. *Cognitive Psychology*, 6(3):380–420.

Roger Brown. 1973. *A first language: The early stages*. Harvard Univ. Press.

Erin Conwell and Katherine Demuth. 2007. Early syntactic productivity: Evidence from dative shift. *Cognition*, 103(2):163–179.

Cynthia Fisher. 2002. The role of abstract syntactic knowledge in language acquisition: A reply to Tomasello. *Cognition*, 82(3):259–278.

A. Kuczaj, Stan. 1977. The acquisition of regular and irregular past tense forms. *Journal of Verbal Learning and Verbal Behavior*, 16(5):589–600.

B. Levin. 1993. *English verb classes and alternations: A preliminary investigation*, volume 348. University of Chicago press Chicago, IL.

Elena Lieven, Dorothé Salomo, and Michael Tomasello. 2009. Two-year-old children's production of multiword utterances: A usage-based analysis. *Cognitive Linguistics*, 20(3):481–507.

B. MacWhinney. 2000. *The CHILDES project: Tools for analyzing talk*, volume 2. Psychology Press.

P. Merlo and S. Stevenson. 2000. Automatic verb classification based on statistical distributions of argument structure. *Computational Linguistics*, 27(3):373–408.

Christopher Parisien and Suzanne Stevenson. 2010. Learning verb alternations in a usage-based bayesian model. In *Proceedings of the 32nd annual meeting of the Cognitive Science Society*.

Amy Perfors, Joshua B. Tenenbaum, and Elizabeth Wonnacott. 2010. Variability, negative evidence, and the acquisition of verb argument constructions. *Journal of Child Language*, 37(03):607–642.

Jacqueline Sachs. 1983. Talking about the There and Then: The emergence of displaced reference in parent–child discourse. *Children's language*, 4.

Sabine Schulte im Walde and Chris Brew. 2002. Inducing German semantic verb classes from purely syntactic subcategorisation information. In *Proceedings of the 40th Annual Meeting of the Association for Computational Linguistics*, pages 223–230, Philadelphia, PA.

Rose M Scott and Cynthia Fisher. 2009. Two-year-olds use distributional cues to interpret transitivity-alternating verbs. *Language and cognitive processes*, 24(6):777–803.

Patrick Suppes. 1974. The semantics of children's language. *American psychologist*, 29(2):103.

Michael Tomasello. 2003. Constructing a language: A usage-based theory of language acquisition.

Michael Tomasello and Kirsten Abbot-Smith. 2002. A tale of two theories: Response to Fisher. *Cognition*, 83(2):207–214.

Elizabeth Wonnacott, Elissa L Newport, and Michael K Tanenhaus. 2008. Acquiring and processing verb argument structure: Distributional learning in a miniature language. *Cognitive psychology*, 56(3):165–209.

A Usage-Based Model of Early Grammatical Development

Barend Beekhuizen
LUCL
Leiden University
b.f.beekhuizen@hum.leidenuniv.nl

Rens Bod
ILLC
University of Amsterdam
l.w.m.bod@uva.nl

Afsaneh Fazly and **Suzanne Stevenson**
Department of Computer Science
University of Toronto
afsaneh,suzanne@cs.toronto.edu

Arie Verhagen
LUCL
Leiden University
a.verhagen@hum.leidenuniv.nl

Abstract

The representations and processes yielding the limited length and telegraphic style of language production early on in acquisition have received little attention in acquisitional modeling. In this paper, we present a model, starting with minimal linguistic representations, that incrementally builds up an inventory of increasingly long and abstract grammatical representations (form+meaning pairings), in line with the usage-based conception of language acquisition. We explore its performance on a comprehension and a generation task, showing that, over time, the model better understands the processed utterances, generates longer utterances, and better expresses the situation these utterances intend to refer to.

1 Introduction

A striking aspect of language acquisition is the difference between children's and adult's utterances. Simulating early grammatical production requires a specification of the nature of the linguistic representations underlying the short, telegraphic utterances of children. In the usage-based view, young children's grammatical represention are thought to be less abstract than adults', e.g. by having stricter constraints on what can be combined with them (cf. Akhtar and Tomasello 1997; Bannard et al. 2009; Ambridge et al. 2012). The representations and processes yielding the restricted length of these early utterances, however, have received little attention. Following Braine (1976), we adopt the working hypothesis that the early learner's grammatical representations are more limited in length (or: arity) than those of adults.

Similarly, in computational modeling of grammar acquisition, comprehension has received more attention than language generation. In this paper we attempt to make the mechanisms underlying early production explicit within a model that can parse and generate utterances, and that incrementally learns constructions (Goldberg, 1995) on the basis of its previous parses. The model's search through the hypothesis space of possible grammatical patterns is highly restricted. Starting from initially small and concrete representations, it learns incrementally long representations (**syntagmatic growth**) as well as more abstract ones (**paradigmatic growth**). Several models address either paradigmatic (Alishahi and Stevenson, 2008; Chang, 2008; Bannard et al., 2009) or syntagmatic (Freudenthal et al., 2010) growth. This model aims to explain both, thereby contributing to the understanding of how different learning mechanisms interact. As opposed to other models involving grammars with semantic representations (Alishahi and Stevenson, 2008; Chang, 2008), but similar to Kwiatkowski et al. (2012), the model starts without an inventory of mappings of single words to meanings.

Based on motivation from usage-based and construction grammar approaches, we define several learning principles that allow the model to build up an inventory of linguistic representations. The model incrementally processes pairs of an utterance U, consisting of a string of words $w_1 \dots w_n$, and a set of situations S, one of which is the situation the speaker intends to refer to. The other situations contribute to propositional uncertainty (the uncertainty over which proposition the speaker is trying to express; Siskind 1996). The model tries to identify the intended situation and to understand how parts of the utterance refer to certain parts of that situation. To do so, the model uses its growing inventory of linguistic representations (Section 2) to analyze U, producing a set of structured semantic analyses or parses (Fig. 1, arrow 1; Section 3).

Proceedings of the 2014 ACL Workshop on Cognitive Modeling and Computational Linguistics, pages 46–54,
Baltimore, Maryland USA, June 26 2014. ©2014 Association for Computational Linguistics

The resulting best parse, U and the selected situation are then stored in a memory buffer (arrow 2), which is used to learn new constructions (arrow 3) using several learning mechanisms (Section 4). The learned constructions can then be used to generate utterances as well. We describe two experiments: in the comprehension experiment (Section 5), we evaluate the model's ability to parse the stream of input items. In the generation experiment (Section 6), the model generates utterances on the basis of a given situation and its linguistic knowledge. We evaluate the generated utterances given different amounts of training items to consider the development of the model over time.

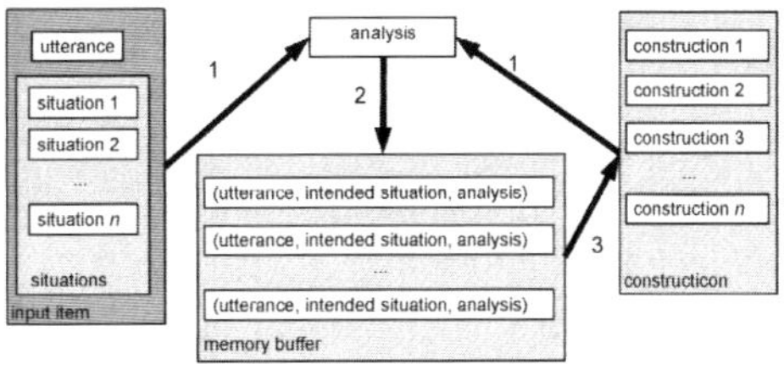

Figure 1: The global flow of the model

2 Representations

We represent linguistic knowledge as **constructions**: pairings of a signifying form and a signified (possibly incomplete) semantic representation (Goldberg, 1995). The **meaning** is represented as a graph with the nodes denoting entities, events, and their relations, connected by directed unlabeled edges. The conceptual content of each node is given by a set of semantic features. We assume that meaning representations are rooted trees. The signifying **form** consists of a positive number of **constituents**. Every constituent has two elements: a phonological form, and a pointer to a node in the signified meaning (in line with Verhagen 2009). Both can be specified, or one can be left empty. Constituents with unspecified phonological forms are called **open**, denoted with ϵ in the figures. The **head constituent** of a construction is defined as the constituent that has a pointer to the root node of the signified meaning. We furthermore require that no two constituents point to the same node of the signified meaning.

This definition generalizes over lexical elements (one phonologically specified constituent) as well as larger linguistic patterns. Fig. 2, for instance, shows two larger constructions being combined with each other. We call the set of constructions the learner has at some moment in time the **constructicon** C (cf. Goldberg 2003).

3 Parsing

3.1 Parsing operations

We first define a **derivation** d as an assembly of constructions in C, using four parsing operations defined below. In parsing, derivations are constrained by the utterance U and the situations S, whereas in production, only a situation s constrains the derivation. The leaf nodes of a derivation must consist of phonological constraints of constructions that (in parsing) are satisfied by U. All constructions used in a derivation must map to the same situation $s \in S$. A construction c maps to s iff the meaning of c constitutes a subgraph of s, with the features on each of the nodes in the meaning of c being a subset of the features on the corresponding node of s. Moreover, each construction must map to a different part of s. This constitutes a mutual exclusivity effect in analyzing U: every part of the analysis must contribute to the composite meaning. A derivation d thus gives us a mapping between the composed meaning of all constructions used in d and one situation $s \in S$. The aggregate mapping specifies a subgraph of s that constitutes the interpretation of that derivation.

The central parsing operation is the COMBINATION operator $\circ$. In $c_i \circ c_j$, the leftmost open constituent of c_i is combined with c_j. Fig. 2 illustrates COMBINATION. COMBINATION succeeds if both the semantic pointer of the leftmost open constituent of c_i and the semantic pointer of the head constituent of c_j map to the same semantic node of a situation s

Initially, the model has few constructions to analyze the utterance with. Therefore, we define three other operations that allow the model to create a derivation over the full utterance without combining constructions. First, a known or unknown word that cannot be fit into a derivation, can be IGNOREd. Second, an unknown word can be used to fill an open constituent slot of a construction with the BOOTSTRAP operator. Bootstrapping entails that the unknown word will be associated with the semantics of the node. Finally, the learner can CONCATENATE multiple derivations, by linearly sequencing them, thus creating a more complex derivation without combining con-

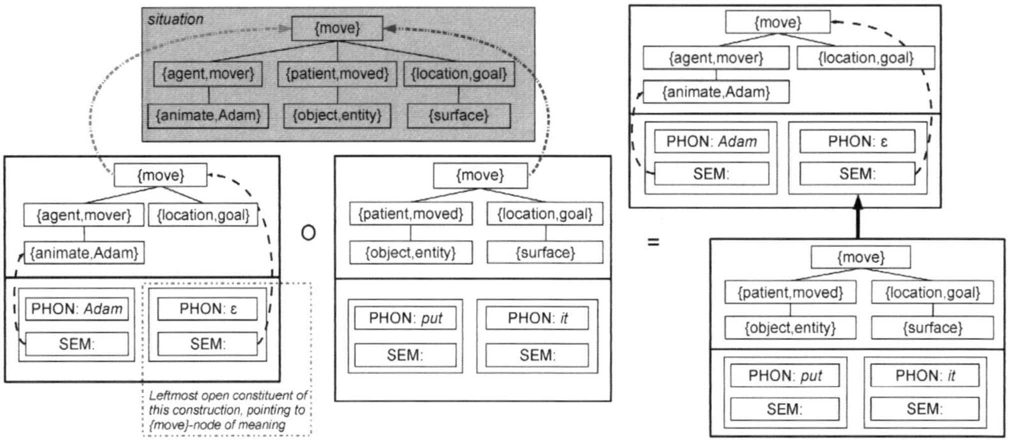

Figure 2: Combining constructions. The dashed lines represent semantic pointers, either from constituents to the constructional meaning (black) or from the constructions to the situation (red and blue).

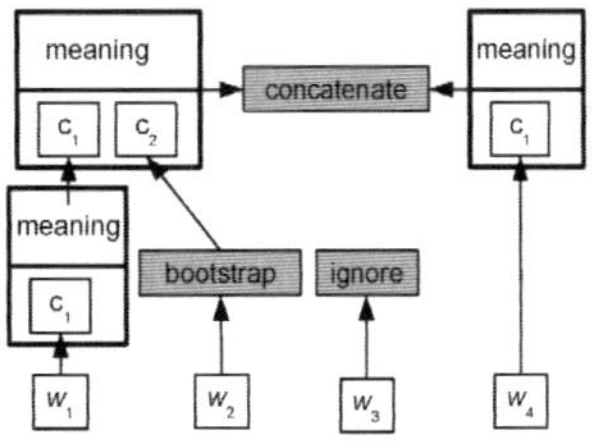

Figure 3: The CONCATENATE, IGNORE and BOOTSTRAP operators (internal details of the constructions left out).

structions. This allows the learner to interpret a larger part of the situation than with COMBINATION only. The resulting sequences may be analyzed in the learning process as constituting one larger construction, consisting of the parts of the concatenated derivations. Fig. 3 illustrates these three operations.

3.2 Selecting the best analysis

Multiple derivations can be highly similar in the way they map parts of U to parts of an $s \in S$. We define a **parse** to be a set of derivations that have the same internal structure and the same mappings to a situation, but that use different constructions in doing so (cf. multiple licensing; Kay 2002). We take the most probable parse of U to be the best analysis of U. The most probable parse points to a situation, which the model then assumes to be the **identified situation** or $s_{\text{identified}}$. If no parse can be made, $s_{\text{identified}}$ is selected at random from S.

The probability of a parse p is given by the sum of the probabilities of the derivations d subsumed under that parse, which in turn are defined as the product of the probabilities of the constructions c used in d.

$$P(p) = \sum_{d \in p} P(d) \tag{1}$$

$$P(d) = \prod_{c \in d} P(c) \tag{2}$$

The probability of a construction $P(c)$ is given by its relative frequency (count) in the construcicon C, smoothed with Laplace smoothing. We assume that the simple parsing operations of IGNORE, BOOTSTRAP, and CONCATENATION reflect usages of an unseen construction with a count of 0.

$$P(c) = \frac{c.count + 1}{\sum_{c' \in C} c'.count + |C| + 1} \tag{3}$$

The most probable parse, U and $s_{\text{identified}}$ are added to the memory buffer. The memory buffer has a pre-set maximal length, discarding the oldest exemplars upon reaching this length. In the future, we plan to consider more realistic mechanisms for the memory buffer, such as graceful degradation, and attention effects.

4 Learning mechanisms

The model uses the best parse of the utterance to develop its knowledge of the constructions in the constructicon C. Two simple operations, UPDATE and ASSOCIATION, are used to create initial constructions and reinforce existing ones respectively. Two additional operations, PARADIGMATIZATION and SYNTAGMATIZATION, are key to the model's ability to extend these initial representations by inducing novel constructions that are richer and more abstract than existing ones.

4.1 Direct learning from the best parse

The best parse is used to UPDATE C. For this mechanism, the model uses the concrete meaning of $s_{\text{identified}}$ rather than the (potentially more abstract) meaning of the constructions in the best parse.[1] Every construction in the parse is assigned the subgraph of $s_{\text{identified}}$ it maps to as its new meaning, and the count of the adjusted construction is incremented with 1, or added to C with a count of 1, if it does not yet exist. This includes applications of the BOOTSTRAP operation, creating a mapping of the previously unknown word to a situational meaning.

ASSOCIATE constitutes a form of simple cross-situational learning over the memory buffer. The intuition is that co-occurring word sequences and meaning components that remain unanalyzed across multiple parses might themselves comprise the form-meaning pairing of a construction. If the unanalyzed parts of two situations contain an overlapping subgraph, and the unanalyzed parts of two utterances an overlapping subsequence of words, the two are mapped to each other and added to C with a count of 0.

4.2 Qualitative extension of the best parse

Syntagmatization Some of the processes described thus far yield analyses of the input in which constructions are linearly associated but lack appropriate relational structure among them. The model requires a process, which we call SYNTAGMATIZATION, that enables it to induce further hierarchical structure.

In order for the learner to acquire constructions in which the different constituents point to different parts of the construction's meaning, the ASSOCIATE operation does not suffice. We assume that the learner is able to learn such constructions by using concatenated derivations. The process we propose is SYNTAGMATIZATION. In this process, the various concatenated derivations are taken as constituents of a novel construction. This instantiates the idea that joint processing of two (or more) events gradually leads to a joint representation of these, previously independent, events.

More precisely, the process starts by taking the top nodes T of the derivations in the best parse, where T consists of the single top node if no CONCATENATION has been applied, or the set of concatenated nodes of the parse tree if CONCATENATION has been applied (e.g. for the derivation in Fig. 3, $|T| = 2$). For each top node $t \in T$, we take the root node of the construction's meaning, and define its **semantic frame** to consist of all children (roles) and grandchildren (role-fillers) of the node in the situation it maps to. The model then forms a novel construction c_{syn} by taking all the constructions in the parse whose semantic root nodes point to a node in this semantic frame, referring to those as the set R of semantically related constructions. As the novel meaning of c_{syn}, the model takes the subgraph of the situation mapped to by the joint mapping of all constructional meanings of constructions in R.

R, as well as all phonologically specified constituents of t itself, are then linearized as the constituents of c_{syn}. The novel construction thus constitutes a construction with a higher arity, 'joining' several previously independent constructions. Fig. 4 illustrates the syntagmatization mechanism.

Paradigmatization Due to our usage-driven approach, all learning mechanisms so far give us maximally concrete constructions. In order for the model to generalize beyond the observed input, some degree of abstraction is needed. The model does so with the PARADIGMATIZATION mechanism. This mechanism recursively looks for minimal abstractions (cf. Tomasello 2003, 123) over the constructions in C and adds those to C, thus creating a full-inheritance network (cf. Langacker 1989, 63-76).

An abstraction over a set of constructions is made if there is an overlapping subgraph between the meanings of the constructions, where every node of the subgraph is the non-empty feature set intersection between two mapped nodes of the constructional meanings. Furthermore, the con-

[1] This follows Langacker's (2009) claim that the processed concrete usage events should leave traces in the learner's mind.

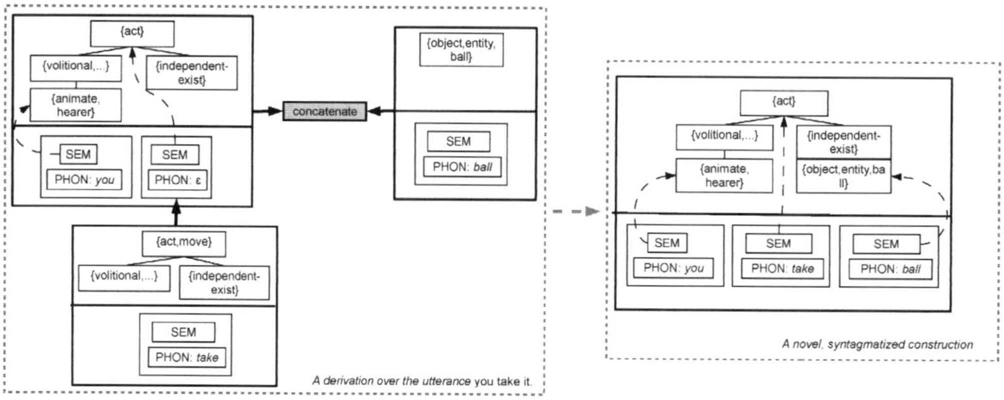

Figure 4: The SYNTAGMATIZATION mechanism. The mechanism takes a derivation as its input and reinterprets it as a novel construction of higher arity).

stituents must be mappable: both constructions have the same number of constituents and the paired constituents point to a mapped node of the meaning. The meaning of the abstracted construction is then set to this overlapping subgraph, which is the lowest possible semantic abstraction over the constructions. The constituents of this new abstraction have a specified phonological form if the more concrete constructions share the same word, and an unspecified one otherwise. The count of an abstracted construction is given by the cardinality of the set of its direct descendants in the network. This generalizes Bybee's (1995) idea about type frequency as a proxy for productivity to a network structure. Fig. 5 illustrates the paradigmatization mechanism.

5 Experimental set-up

The model is incrementally presented with U, S pairings based on Alishahi & Stevenson's (2010) generation procedure. In this procedure, an utterance and a semantic frame expressing its meaning (a situation) are generated. The generation procedure follows distributions occurring in a corpus of child-directed speech. As we are interested in the performance of the model under propositional uncertainty, we add a parametrized number of randomly sampled situations, so that S consists of the situation the speaker intends to refer to (s_{correct}) and a number of situations the speaker does not intend to refer to.[2] Here, we set the number of additional situations to be 1 or 5; the other parameter of the model, the size of the memory buffer, is set to 5 exemplars.

For the **comprehension** experiment, we evaluate the model's performance parsing the input items, averaging over every 50 U, S pairs. We track the ability to **identify** the intended situation from S. Identification succeeds if the best parse maps to s_{correct}, i.e. if $s_{\text{identified}} = s_{\text{correct}}$. Next, **situation coverage** expresses what proportion of $s_{\text{identified}}$ has been interpreted and thus how rich the meanings of the used constructions are. It is defined as the number of nodes of the interpretation of the best parse, divided by the number of nodes of $s_{\text{identified}}$. Finally, **utterance coverage** tells us what proportion of U has been parsed with constructions (excluding IGNORED; including BOOTSTRAPPED words). The measure expresses the proportion of the signal that the learner (correctly or incorrectly) is able to interpret.

For exploring language **production**, the model receives a situation, and (given the constructicon) finds the most probable, maximally expressive, fully lexicalized derivation expressing it. That is: among all derivations terminating in phonologically specified constituents, it selects the derivations that cover the most semantic nodes of the given situation. In the case of multiple such derivations, it selects the most probable one, following the probability model in Section 3. We only allow for the COMBINATION operator in the derivations, as BOOTSTRAPPING and IGNORE re-

[2]We are currently researching the effects of sampling non-correct situations that have a greater likelihood of overlap with the intended situation, to reflect more realistic input (cf. Siskind 1996).

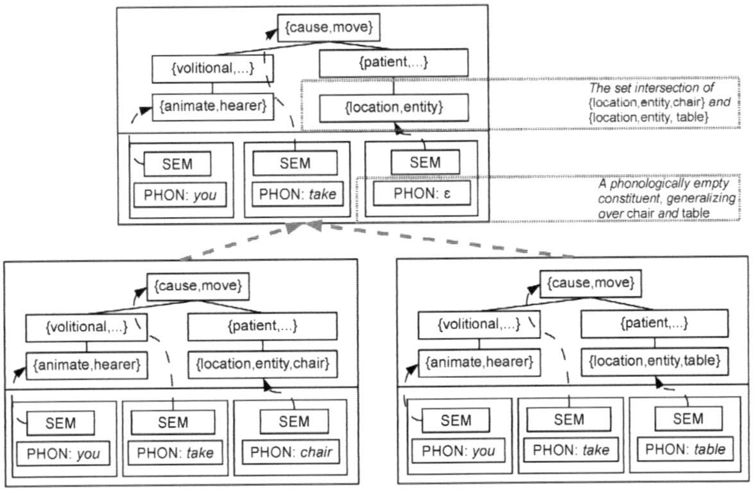

Figure 5: The PARADIGMATIZATION mechanism. The construction on top is an abstraction obtained over the two constructions at the bottom.

fer to words in a given U, and CONCATENATE is a back-off method for analyzing more of U than the constructicon allows for. The situations used in the generation experiment do not occur in the training items, so that we truly measure the model's ability to generate utterances for novel situations.

The phonologically specified leaf nodes of the best derivation constitute the generated utterance U_{gen}. U_{gen} is evaluated on the basis of its **mean length**, in number of words, its **situation coverage**, as defined in the comprehension experiment, and its **utterance precision** and **utterance recall**. To calculate these, we take the maximally overlapping subsequence U_{overlap} between the actual utterance U_{act} associated with the situation and U_{gen}. Utterance precision (how many words are generated correctly) and utterance recall (how many of the correct words are generated) are defined as:

$$\text{Utterance precision} = \frac{|U_{\text{overlap}}|}{|U_{\text{gen}}|} \quad (4)$$

$$\text{Utterance recall} = \frac{|U_{\text{overlap}}|}{|U_{\text{act}}|} \quad (5)$$

Because the U, S-pairs on which the model was trained, are generated randomly, we show results for comprehension and production averaged over 5 simulations.

6 Experiments

A central motivation for the development of this model is to account for early grammatical production: can we simulate the developmental pattern of the growth of utterance length and a growing potential for generalization? The same constructions underlying these productions should, at the same time, also account for the learner's increasing grasp of the meaning of U. To explore the model's performance in both domains, we present a comprehension and a generation experiment.

6.1 Comprehension results

Fig. 6a gives us the results over time of the comprehension measures given a propositional uncertainty of 1, i.e. one situation besides s_{correct} in S. Overall, the model understands the utterances increasingly well. After 2000 input items, the model identifies s_{correct} in 95% of the cases. With higher levels of propositional uncertainty (not shown here), performance is still relatively robust: given 5 incorrect situations in S, s_{correct} is identified in 62% of all cases (random guessing gives a score of 17%, or $\frac{1}{6}$). Similarly, the proportion of the situation interpreted and the proportion of the utterance analyzed go up over time. This means that the model builds up an increasing repertoire of constructions that allow it to analyze larger parts of the utterance and the situations it identifies. It is important to realize that these mea-

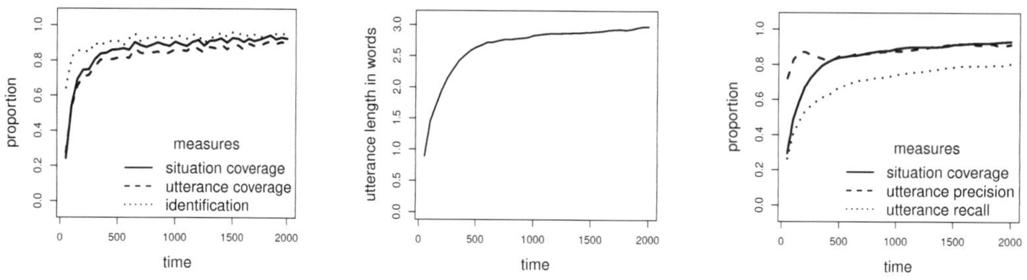

(a) Comprehension results over time (b) Length of U_{gen} over time (c) Generation results over time

Figure 6: Quantitative results for the comprehension and generation experiments

sures do not display what proportion of the utterance or situation is analyzed correctly.

6.2 Generation results

Quantitative results Fig. 6b shows that the average utterance length increases over time. This indicates that the number of constituents of the used constructions grows. Next, Fig. 6c shows the performance of the model on the generation task. After 2000 input items, the model generates productions expressing 93% of the situation, with an utterance precision of 0.91, and an utterance recall of 0.81. Given a propositional uncertainty of 5, these go down to 79%, 0.76 and 0.59 respectively.

Comparing the utterance precision and recall over time, we can see that the utterance precision is high from the start, whereas the recall gradually increases. This is in line with the observation that children predominantly produce errors of omission (leaving linguistic material out an adult speaker would produce), and few errors of comission (producing linguistic material an adult speaker would not produce).

Qualitative results Tracking individual productions given specific situations over time allows us to study in detail what the model is doing. Here, we look at one case qualitatively. Given the situation for which the U_{act} is *she put them away*, the model generates, over time, the utterances in Table 1. The brackets show the internal hierarchical structure of the derivation. This development illustrates several interesting aspects of the model. First, as discussed earlier, the model mostly makes errors of omission: earlier productions leave out more words found in the adult utterances. Only at $t = 550$, the model makes an error of commission, using the word *in* erroneously.

	[[she] put]	[she [put]]	[[she] [put] [in]]	[[she] put them [away]]	[[she] put [them]]	[[she] put them [away]]	[[she] put [them] away]	[[she] put them away]
t	50	500	550	600	950	1000	1050	1400

Table 1: Generations over time t for one situation.

Starting from $t = 600$ (except at $t = 950$), the model generates the correct utterance, but the derivations leading to this production differ. At $t = 550$, for instance, the learner combines a completely non-phonologically specific construction for which the constituents refer to the agent, action and goal location, with three 'lexical' constructions that fill in the words for those items.. The constructions used after $t = 550$ are all more specific, combining 3, or even only 2 constructions ($t \geq 1400$) where the entire sequence of words "put them away" arises from a single construction.

Using less abstract constructions over time seems contrary to the usage-based idea that constructions become more abstract over the course of acquisition. However, this result follows from the way the probability model is defined. More specific constructions that are able to account for the input will entail fewer combinations, and a derivation with fewer combination operations will often be more likely than one with more such operations. Given equal expressivity of the situation, the former derivation will be selected over the latter in generation.

The effect is indeed in line with another concept hypothesized to play a role in language acquisition on a usage-based account, viz. pre-emption (Gold-

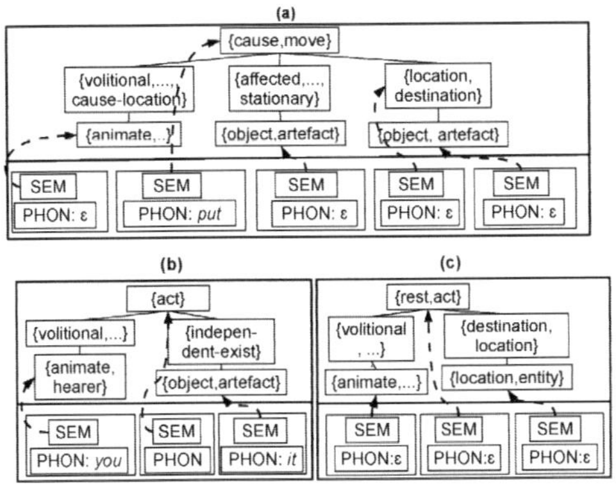

Figure 7: Some representations at $t = 2000$

berg, 2006, 94-95). Pre-emption is the effect that a language user will select a more concrete representation over the combination of more abstract ones. The effect can be reconceptualized in this model as an epiphenomenon of the way the probability model works: simply because combining fewer constructions in a derivation is often more probable than combining more constructions, the former derivation will be selected over the latter. Pre-emption is typically invoked to explain the blocking of overgeneralization patterns, and an interesting future step will be to see if the model can simulate developmental patterns for well-known cases of overgeneralization errors.

The potential for abstraction The paradigmatization operation allows the model to go beyond observed concrete instances of form-meaning pairings: without it, unseen situations could never be fully expressed. Despite this potential, we have seen that the model relies on highly concrete constructions. The concreteness of the used patterns, however, does not imply the absence of more abstract representations. Fig. 7 gives three examples of constructions in C in one simulation. Construction (a) could be seen as a verb-island construction (Tomasello, 1992, 23-24). The second constituent is phonologically specified with *put*, and the other arguments are open, but mapped to specific semantic functions. This pattern allows for the expression of many caused-motion events. Construction (b) is the inverse of (a): the arguments are phonologically specified, but the verb-slot is open. This would be a case of a pronominal argument frame [*you* V *it*], which have been found to be helpful in the bootstrapping of verbal meanings (Tomasello, 2001). Finally, (c) presents a case of full abstraction. This construction licenses utterances such as *I sit here*, *you stay there* and erroneous ones like *he sits on* (which, again, will be pre-empted in the generation of utterances if more concrete constructions licence *he sits on it*).

Summarizing, abstract constructions are acquired, but only used for those cases in which no concrete construction is available. This is in line with the usage-based hypotheses that abstract constructions do emerge, but that for much of language production, a language user can rely on highly concrete patterns. A next step will be to measure the development of abstractness and length over the constructions themselves, rather than the parses and generations they allow.

7 Conclusion

This, admittedly complex, model forms an attempt to model different learning mechanisms in interaction from a usage-based constructionist perspective. Starting with an empty set of linguistic representations, the model acquires words and grammatical constructions simultaneously. The learning mechanisms allow the model to build up increasingly **abstract**, as well as increasingly **long** constructions. With these developing representations, we showed how the model gets better over time at understanding the input item, performing relatively robustly under propositional uncertainty.

Moreover, in the generation experiment, the model shows patterns of production (increasingly long utterances) similar to those of children. An important future step will be to look at these productions more closely and investigate if they also converge on more detailed patterns of development in the production of children (e.g. item-specificity, as hypothesized on the usage-based view). Despite highly concrete constructions sufficing for most of production, inspection of the acquired representations tells us that more abstract constructions are learned as well. Here, an interesting next step would be to simulate patterns of overgeneralization in children's production.

Acknowledgements

We would like to thank three anonymous reviewers for their valuable and thoughtful comments. We gratefully acknowledge the funding of BB through NWO of the Netherlands (322.70.001) and AF and SS through NSERC of Canada.

References

Nameera Akhtar and Michael Tomasello. 1997. Young Children's Productivity With Word Order and Verb Morphology. *Developmental Psychology*, 33(6):952–965.

Afra Alishahi and Suzanne Stevenson. 2008 A Computational Model of Early Argument Structure Acquisition. *Cognitive Science*, 32(5):789–834.

Afra Alishahi and Suzanne Stevenson. 2010. A computational model of learning semantic roles from child-directed language. *Language and Cognitive Processes*, 25(1):50–93.

Ben Ambridge, Julian M Pine, and Caroline F Rowland. 2012. Semantics versus statistics in the retreat from locative overgeneralization errors. *Cognition*, 123(2):260–79.

Colin Bannard, Elena Lieven, and Michael Tomasello. 2009. Modeling children's early grammatical knowledge. *Proceedings of the National Academy of Sciences of the United States of America*, 106(41):17284–9.

Martin D.S. Braine. 1976. *Children's first word combinations*. University of Chicago Press, Chicago, IL.

Joan Bybee. 1995. Regular morphology and the lexicon. *Language and Cognitive Processes*, 10 (5):425–455.

Nancy C.-L. Chang. 2008. *Constructing Grammar: A computational model of the emergence of early constructions*. Dissertation, University of California, Berkeley.

Daniel Freudenthal, Julian Pine, and Fernand Gobet. 2010. Explaining quantitative variation in the rate of Optional Infinitive errors across languages: a comparison of MOSAIC and the Variational Learning Model. *Journal of Child Language*, 37(3):643–69.

Adele E. Goldberg. 1995. *Constructions. A Construction Grammar Approach to Argument Structure.* Chicago University Press, Chicago, IL.

Adele E Goldberg. 2003. Constructions: a new theoretical approach to language. *Trends in Cognitive Sciences*, 7(5):219–224.

Adele E. Goldberg. 2006. *Constructions at Work. The Nature of Generalization in Language*. Oxford University Press, Oxford.

Paul Kay. 2002. An Informal Sketch of a Formal Architecture for Construction Grammar. *Grammars*, 5:1–19.

Tom Kwiatkowski, Sharon Goldwater, Luke Zettlemoyer, and Mark Steedman. 2012. A Probabilistic Model of Syntactic and Semantic Acquisition from Child-Directed Utterances and their Meanings. In *Proceedings EACL*.

Ronald W. Langacker. 1989. *Foundations of Cognitive Grammar, Volume I.* Stanford University Press.

Ronald W. Langacker. 2009. A dynamic view of usage and language acquisition. *Cognitive Linguistics*, 20(3):627–640.

Jeffrey M Siskind. 1996. A computational study of cross-situational techniques for learning word-to-meaning mappings. *Cognition*, 61(1-2):39–91.

Michael Tomasello. 1992. *First Verbs: A study of early grammatical development*. Cambridge University Press, Cambridge, UK.

Michael Tomasello. 2001 Perceiving intentions and learning words in the second year of life. In Melissa Bowerman and Stephen C. Levinson, editors, *Language Acquisition and Conceptual Development*, chapter 5, pages 132–158. Cambridge University Press, Cambridge, UK.

Michael Tomasello. 2003. *Constructing a language: A Usage-Based Theory of Language Acquisition*. Harvard University Press, Cambridge, MA.

Arie Verhagen. 2009 The conception of constructions as complex signs. Emergence of structure and reduction to usage. *Constructions and Frames*, 1:119–152.

Linguistic Adaptation in Conversation Threads: Analyzing Alignment in Online Health Communities

Yafei Wang, David Reitter, and John Yen
Information Science and Technology
Penn State University
University Park, PA, 16801
yxw184@ist.psu.edu, reitter@psu.edu, jyen@ist.psu.edu

Abstract

Previous studies of alignment have focused on two-party conversations. We study multi-party conversation in online health communities, which have shown benefits for their members from forum conversations. So far, our understanding of the relationship between alignment in such multi-party conversations and its possible connection to member benefits has been limited. This paper quantifies linguistic alignment in the oldest and the largest cancer online forum. Alignment at lexical and syntactic levels, as well as decay of alignment was observed in forum threads, although the decay was slower than commonly found in psycholinguistic studies. The different pattern of adaptation to the initial post on a thread suggests that specific roles in the online forum (e.g., seeking support from the community) can potentially be revealed through alignment theory and its extensions.

1 Introduction

Linguistic alignment leads conversation partners to adapt their language patterns to match their conversation partners. Such patterns comprise of word choice, sentence structure, and more. For example, if one conversation partner uses passive voice in the conversation, other conversation participants tend to use passive voice at a later point in time. The mechanism of adaptation are better understood now (Bock and Griffin, 2000; Pickering and Ferreira, 2008; Kaschak et al., 2011a; Reitter et al., 2011). The Interactive Alignment Model (IAM) (Pickering and Garrod, 2004) attributes dialogic function to the priming effect; it suggests that adaptation helps people reach mutual understanding. Some recent studies (Reitter and Moore, 2007; Fusaroli et al., 2012) lend empirical confirmation to this thesis.

Repetition effects are not purely mechanistic. They are sometimes moderated in response to situational requirements or framing. For example, they can vary in strength when humans (believe to) communicate with computers (Branigan et al., 2010). Repetition intensifies when the purpose of conversation is to collaborate on a common task (Reitter et al., 2006). Of course, communication between individuals is more than a linguistic event; it is also social. For example, it can be found as a cue to social relationships in film scripts (Danescu-Niculescu-Mizil and Lee, 2011). A more specific aspect of language-based interaction is pragmatic convention in multi-party dialogue, which determines turn-taking, shifts in topic, and more.

One would expect alignment to also occur in social situations involving multiple speakers. The social moderators and functions of adaptation effects, however, are largely unclear. The question we ask in this paper is whether alignment is moderated by the role of a speaker's contribution to the conversation. In this paper, we deal with written interaction only; our data are internet forum conversations.

The first question is whether linguistic adaptation exists in online communities and online groups. Dialogues in threads of online communities are different from previous types of dialogues. Unlike some spontaneous, free-form dialogues, threaded conversations have specific topic. In addition, thread conversations do not have specific tasks. Therefore, we investigate whether dialogues in the threads also exhibit linguistic adaptation, be it as an artifact of mechanistic language processing or because adaptation acts as a social or conversational signal. Adaptation tends to decay over time, although this decay has not been studied in the context of such

Proceedings of the 2014 ACL Workshop on Cognitive Modeling and Computational Linguistics, pages 55–62,
Baltimore, Maryland USA, June 26 2014. ©2014 Association for Computational Linguistics

slow, asychronuous communication. Therefore, we will characterize the time-scale of dacay. More generally, if alignment exists in forums, is it correlated with the communicative role of a text or the social role of its author?

The contributions of this paper are: (1) an exploratory analysis of linguistic adaptation based on 3,000 conversations threads and 23,045 posts in an online cancer survivor community (`http://csn.cancer.org`). Specifically, we find reliable linguistic adaptation effects in this corpus. (2) We show that properties of conversation threads that are different from regular conversations.

In the following sections, we first survey related work on linguistic adaptation. Then, we describe our data and make preliminary definitions. We then introduce measures of linguistic adaptation. Last, we discuss a set of properties in online thread conversations which are unlike other types of dialogues.

2 Related Work

Linguistic alignment phenomenon in social interaction has been well explored in previous literature. It happens because of multiple reasons. Firstly, it could be due to unconscious linguistic adaptation. Pickering and Garrod (2004) suggests that conversations have linguistic coordination at lexical level. Branigan et al. (2000) and Gries (2005) show that priming effects exist at the syntactic level. However, linguistic alignment could happen consciously by conversation participants. Some literature suggest that people flexibly adapt their linguistic patterns to each other's in order to improve collective performance and social coordination (Healey and Mills, 2006; Garrod and Pickering, 2009).

Linguistic alignment has been found in written communication as well, which is close to our work. Danescu-Niculescu-Mizil et al. (2011) examines conversations in a Twitter corpus, showing convergence of Linguistic Inquiry and Word Count (LIWC) measures. This result confirms that linguistic alignment exists in written online social media. Furthermore, in Huffaker et al. (2006); Scissors et al. (2008); Backstrom et al. (2013) also show that people adjust their linguistic style, such as linguistic features, in the online written chatroom and online community. Also, priming effects at syntactic level (Gries, 2005; Branigan et al., 2000) have been explored in several written dataset settings (Pickering and Ferreira, 2008).

In order to quantify the linguistic alignment phenomenon, researchers have introduced several quantitative measures. Several methods evaluate repetition of linguistic events, such as the use of words, syntactic rules or a small set of expressions (Church, 2000; Reitter et al., 2006; Fusaroli et al., 2012). These approaches typically test whether linguistic alignment is due to linguistic adaptation or intrinsic repetition. Moreover, linguistic feature similarity (Stenchikova and Stent, 2007; Danescu-Niculescu-Mizil et al., 2011) is also widely used to measure linguistic adaptation precisely.

3 Online Health Communities

Online health communities (OHC) typically include features such as discussion boards where cancer survivors and their caregivers can interact with each other. Support and information from people with similar cancers or problems is very valuable because cancer experiences are unique. Therefore, an online community for cancer survivors and caregivers enables them to share experiences related to cancer, seek solutions to daily living issues, and in general support one another (Bambina, 2007) in ways that is not often possible with other close family, friends or even health care providers. Benefits to cancer survivors who have participated in an OHC are reported in the literature. Studies of cancer OHC have indicated that participation increases social support (Dunkel-Schetter, 1984; Rodgers and Chen, 2005), reduces levels of stress, depression, and psychological trauma (Beaudoin and Tao, 2008; Winzelberg et al., 2003), and helps participants be more optimistic about the course of their life with cancer (Rodgers and Chen, 2005). The support received from other OHC members help cancer patients better cope with their disease and improve their lives both physically and mentally (Dunkel-Schetter, 1984). Further understanding about these benefits has been provided by computational text analysis and machine learning methods, which enable fine-grained analysis of the sentiments of individual posts in the discussion forum of cancer OHC Qiu et al. (2011). It has been shown that those who started a thread in a cancer OHC often show a more positive sentiment in their posts later in the thread, after other OHC members provided replies Qiu et al. (2011); Portier et al. (2013). However, the potential relationship between alignment theory and these benefits of cancer OHC has not been explored. This motivates us to study the alignment of posts on a thread to the initial post that starts the thread.

4 Data Description and Preliminary Definitions

The data used in this study stem from the Cancer Survivor's Network (CSN) (`http://csn.cancer.org`). The CSN is the oldest and the largest cancer online community for cancer survivors, which includes cancer patients, and their friends and families. CSN has more than 166,000 members (Portier et al., 2013). Members in CSN present their concerns, ask questions, share their personal experience and provide social support to each other through discussion threads. Similar to other online communities, CSN threads consist of an initial post followed by a sequence of reply posts ordered by time. A thread could be represented as a sequence of post, $< P_1, P_2, \cdots, P_i, \cdots, P_n >$. In order to better explain the problem, we show some properties of a post in the thread.

Absolute Position: Given a post P_i in a thread, the absolute position of post P_i is *i*

Relative Position: Given a post P_i in a thread with n posts, the relative position of P_i is *i/n*

We construct the CSN corpus by randomly sampling 3,000 threads from CSN between 2000 and 2010. Using Stanford's CoreNLP tool (Klein and Manning, 2003), we generate the syntactic structure of the text in each post. In order to calculate linguistic adaptation, we convert every syntactic tree into structure rules in phrases (Reitter et al., 2006). The data distribution of CSN corpus is shown in Figure 1.

5 Measures of Linguistic Adaptation

Following previous work, we implement *Indiscriminate Local Linguistic Alignment* (Fusaroli et al., 2012) at the levels of syntax and lexicon. In general, indiscriminate local linguistic alignment measures the repetition of language use in the target post repeating prime posts. LILA, as defined, is a normalized measure of the number of words that occur in both the prime and the target.

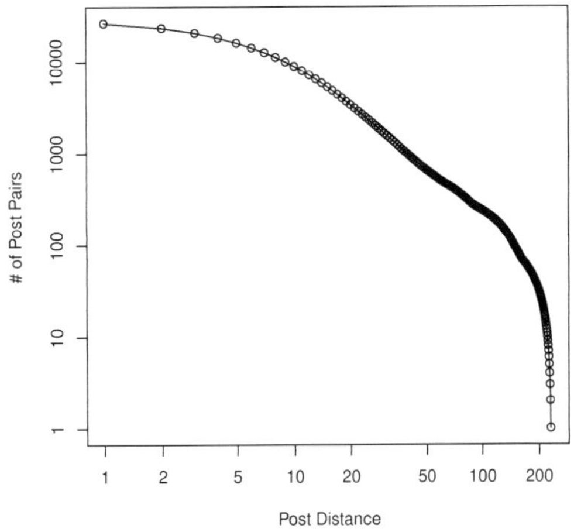

Figure 1: The distribution of posts based on post distance.

The normalization factor is the product of the length of the prime and the length of the target.

Alignment has been demonstrated for syntax and lexicon, ranging from controlled experimentation to broad-coverage naturalistic text (e.g., Bock, 1986; Gries, 2005; Ferreira and Bock, 2006; Reitter et al., 2006). In this paper, we present primarily exploratory analyses that emphasize minimal filtering and data processing. While some priming effects discussed in the literature indeed require careful post-hoc control using many explanatory variables, the phenomena we discuss are evident with exploratory, early-stage methods.

5.1 Indiscriminate local linguistic alignment at the lexical level

Lexical Indiscriminate Local Linguistic Alignment (LILLA) measures word repetition between one or more *prime* post and a *target* post. The prime always precedes the target. LILLA, in our implementation, can be seen as the probability of a word occurring in a single location, given it occurred in a prime period. Formally,

$$\text{LILLA}(target, prime) = \frac{p(target|prime)}{p(target)} \tag{1}$$

$$= \frac{\sum_{word_i \epsilon target} \delta(word_i)}{length(prime) * length(target)} \tag{2}$$

$$\delta(word_i) = \begin{cases} 1 & \text{if word}_i \in \text{prime} \\ 0 & otherwise \end{cases} \quad (3)$$

where length(X) is the number of words in post X, and target post is any post following the prime post. The distance between the two posts is measured in posts. In different experiment settings, we focus on certain prime posts, such as the first post of a thread, or all posts written by a certain author.

To sum up, LILLA is measured as word repetition conditioned on the word having been primed in a previous post. A high value of LILLA indicates an increased level of linguistic alignment. Alignment at the lexical level can have a number of underlying causes, including lexical priming, but also simply topicality of the posts. Therefore, it is important to also inspect indiscriminate local linguistic alignment at the syntactic level.

5.2 Indiscriminate local linguistic alignment at the syntactic level

Here, we consider a priming effect of syntactic structure, which shows users' implicit linguistic adaptation. Similar to Reitter et al. (2006), our cancer survivor network corpus was annotated with phrase structure trees; unlike in previous work, we do so using a parser (from the Stanford CoreNLP package (Klein and Manning, 2003)). Each post is encoded as a series of syntactic rules. *Indiscriminate local linguistic alignment at the syntactic level* (SILLA) measures the repetition of syntactic rules in the target post. Similar to our experiments in lexical repetition, prime posts will vary in different experimental settings.

5.3 Alignment and Adaptation

In this paper, we distinguish *alignment* and *adaptation*. Alignment is the general adoption of words, phrases, syntax, and any linguistic representation that was heard, read, spoken or written previously. Adaptation is a special case of alignment: here, speakers permanently adjust their linguistic preferences, or they *learn* from their linguistic experiences. Alignment can be due to a memory effect (e.g., priming), while adaptation may alternatively be the result of speakers discussing a topic. When they do, they are more likely to use the same words. Both alignment and adaptation may decay over time.

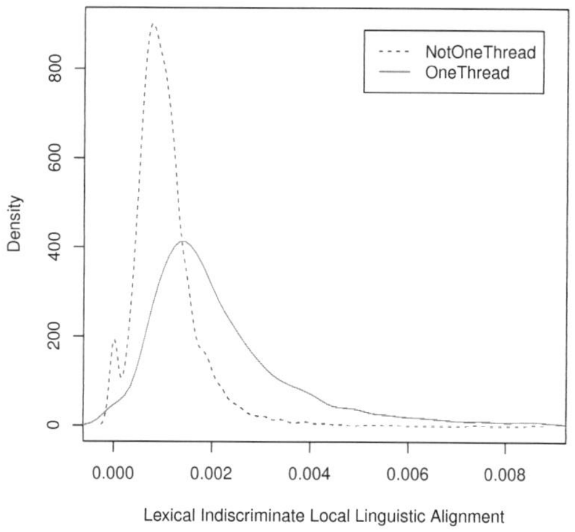

Figure 2: Distribution of lexical indiscriminate local linguistic alignment compared to a control (NotOneThread).

6 Linguistic properties of conversation threads

In this section, we will set up four experiments to show the alignment properties of conversation threads. For simplification, we will only consider replies whose post distance is less than 100 (data distribution shown in Figure 1).

6.1 Linguistic alignment

We assume that there is a constant level of random indiscriminate local linguistic repetition in human language, both lexically and syntactically.

We designed a post-hoc experiment to test whether linguistic alignment effect is due to linguistic adaptation or intrinsic repetition in human language, following methodology to measure long-term adaptation developed in Reitter and Moore (2007). We split each of 3,000 threads into two equal-size (by posts) halves. Out of the resulting 6,000 thread halves, we produce pairs combining any two sampled thread halves.

We define the binary OneThread variable, indicating whether a pair consists of material from the same thread, or if it consists of a first half from one thread, but a second half from another thread. This allows us to contrast repetition within and between threads. If linguistic adaptation exist, linguistic repetition at the lexical and syntactic levels between the two halves of a pair will be

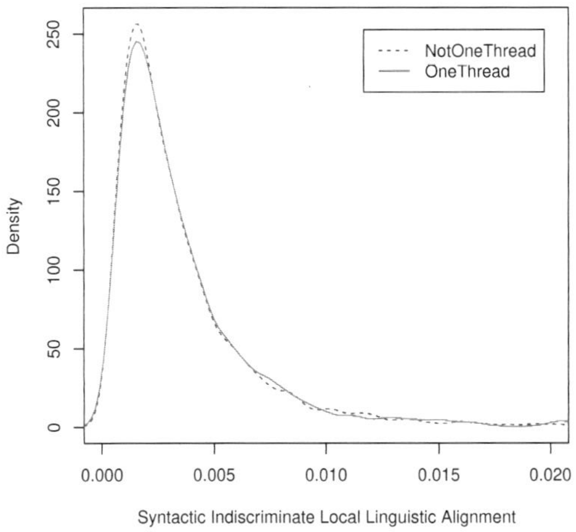

Figure 3: Distribution of syntactic indiscriminate local linguistic alignment compared to a control (NotOneThread).

more common if OneThread is true.

Figures 2 and 3 show that linguistic repetition in the same thread is greater than the control (repetition between different threads) (Wilcoxon-test $p_{LILLA} < 0.001$, $p_{SILLA} < 0.001$). However, despite the statistical difference, it is obvious that there is a strong lexical alignment effect, but much less syntactic alignment. As a result, we conclude that at least some linguistic repetition in the online conversation is due to linguistic adaptation. Again, at the lexical level, we would expect some of this repetition to be due to the preferred repetition of topical words; at the syntactic level, this is unlikely to be the case.

6.2 Linguistic Adaptation Decays

Strong syntactic repetition has been shown to diminish within seconds (Reitter et al., 2006). Precisely, given an use of a syntactic construction at one point in time, the probability of this construction being used again is strongly increased for the first seconds, but decays rapidly towards its prior probability. In our experiment, we replicate the decay of linguistic repetition at the larger scale of forum threads. From a psycholinguistic perspective, one would expect only a relatively weak effect, given that syntactic short-term priming is often short-lived (Branigan et al., 1999). However, there is also weaker, slow, long-term persistence (Bock and Griffin, 2000), which can even be cumulative (Jaeger and Snider, 2007; Kaschak et al., 2011b). The messages in such forums are written at a much larger timescale than the priming models and short-term priming lab experiments investigate.

In the experiment, we split a thread into a sequence of posts. Given a target post P_j, the prime post is one post in the subsequence of posts $< P_1, \cdots, P_i, \cdots, P_{j-1} >$. We calculate LILLA and SILLA of posts for prime-target distances below 100. We will use the same method in this and following experiments.

Figures 4 and 5 show that LILLA and SILLA drop as the post-distance between a target post and a prime post in the thread increases. Comparing syntactic and lexical decay, we note that the slope of LILLA's decay is stronger than that of SILLA's decay. Both two measurements imply that linguistic alignment decays over time, by "utterance" (for some definition of utterance), or by post. These results parallel standard results from the priming literature. Surprisingly, for forum threads we find this effect at a much larger scale than in one-on-one spoken dialogue.

6.3 Linguistic adaptation to the initial post

So far, we have largely replicated a known alignment effect for the case of written communication in the online forum. There are some properties of the forum communication that allow us to investigate a number of open questions pertaining to alignment in multi-party dialogue. The main question concerns the function of alignment. Is it more than an artifact of low-level memory effects (priming)? Does it, as Pickering and Garrod (2004) have argued, contribute to mutual understanding? Or is it, beyond that, a mechanism to express or establish social relationships? If alignment is not just a purely functional phenomenon, but also carries pragmatic weight or social functions, we would not expect it to be blind to the role of the author of the source (prime) post.

In a self-help online discussion forum, the role of the initial post differs from that of other messages. The initial post raises an issue generally, or it poses a concrete question. In this experiment, we test whether initial posts in the thread are more important than other replies

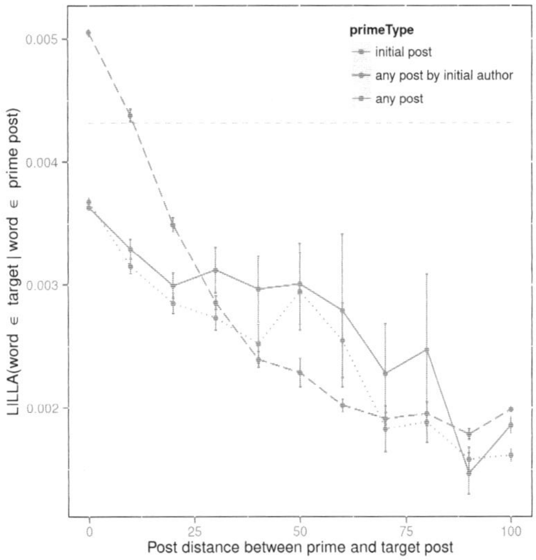

Figure 4: **Lexical** indiscriminate local linguistic adaptation to any post, the initial post and the posts from the initial author of the thread. The light gray horizontal line shows the mean LILLA to any post in the thread. Error bars: standard errors. (The dashed horizontal line shows the prior, which is large due to the large number of many short threads.)

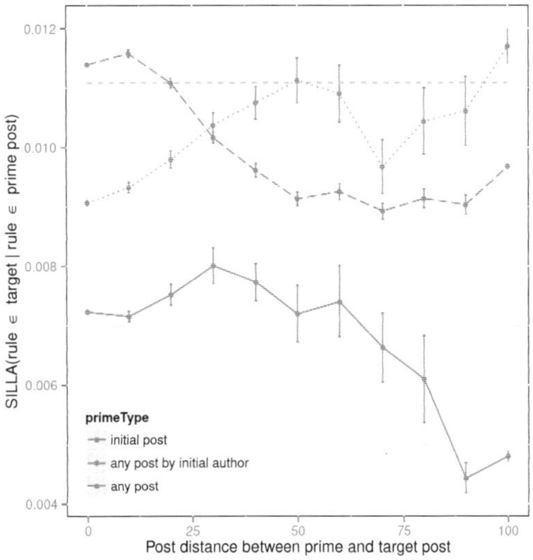

Figure 5: **Syntactic** indiscriminate local linguistic adaptation to any post, the initial post, and the posts from the initial author in the thread. The light gray horizontal line shows the mean SILLA to any post in the thread.

in online conversations. That is, given an initial post, does linguistic alignment still decline with increasing post distance between the initial post and the reply post in the online discussion thread? Also, is linguistic alignment to the initial post higher than that to any post?

Figure 4 plots lexical alignment (LILLA). We can see that lexical alignment is present for the initial post as well, but not more so than in general. In fact, the absolute level as well as the decay of LILLA to the initial post is weaker than that of LILLA to any post in the thread.

To distinguish linguistic adaptation from more general alignment effects, we also test syntactic alignment, SILLA. Figure 5 plots this measure. SILLA shows a different story compared to LILLA. It shows that syntactic adaptation takes place (and decays) for all posts, but that there is less, if even initial anti-alignment with the posts from the initial author. The results may be supported by properties of conversation in internet threads. In an online community, initial posts generally raise questions. Different sentence types (e.g., questions) may be used by someone seeking help. So, alignment with the initial post may seem to decay after post 25, but also shows more variance (due to fewer data-points).

In sum, both measurements suggest that linguistic alignment takes place with general material presented before the target text, and that repetition probability does decrease over time or linguistic material (posts) as theoretically predicted. We do not see evidence for a strong social role of alignment.

6.4 Linguistic adaptation to the author of the first post

As the previous experiment showed, lexical alignment to the initial post decays over time. There is no evidence that alignment with the initial post is related to its informational role in the thread. However, is alignment affected by the social role taken on by the author that asks the initial question? In other words, do writers align more with posts from the initial author than with others?

Figure 4 shows that LILLA drops gradually when prime posts are restricted to the initial author. Lexical alignment to the initial author behaves similarly to alignment with the initial post. At the lexical level, repetition of material provided by the initial author or initial post does not drop as rapidly as it does for general material, and it starts at a lower level. Further investigations will be needed to better understand the alignment effects and the slow decay with the thread-initiating post. For example, further analysis is needed to investigate whether the slow decay is related to the support function the community provides to the thread initiators. Syntactic alignment (SILLA, Figure 5) suggests weaker alignment effects for the initial author and the initial post. Further investigations will also be needed to study the syntactic alignment of replying posts to early reply posts. If such alignment exists, it provides further insights about the leadership role in the community (Zhao et al., 2014).

This finding result may be supported by properties of online support communities. Specifically, the author of the initial post is the person that would like to receive support from other community members. People who reply provide support to that initial author. Therefore, replies in the thread are likely to have expressions different from those used in the initial post and by the initial author.

7 Conclusion

Motivated by analyzing linguistic adaptation behavior in online communities, we provide a descriptive analysis that qualifies linguistic alignment at both the lexical and syntactic levels. A novel observation is that we find reliable linguistic adaptation in online communities. We replicate the temporal, logarithmic decay, but we found it at a much slower pace or larger scale than psycholinguistic work has done in experiment or corpus studies.

The distinction we make between syntactic and lexical alignment has implications for the possible mechanisms behind the adaptation effect. A writer's lexical choices are influenced by topic, while syntactic composition happens implicitly, i.e., without (conscious) attention. Topics do not remain the same during a conversation: they shift throughout the thread. This clustering of topics can create alignment and decay but as far as permanent adaptation is concerned there is nothing but the illusion of it.

Our study provides some insight into properties of linguistic alignment particularly in thread-based discussions. Different from regular dialogues, the initial post and the author of the initial post may have a special role in such dialogues. We see differences in lexical and syntactic alignment. We assume that these are likely due to conversational properties rather than underlying cognitive processes.

This phenomenon provides an interesting angle to study online communities as well as linguistic alignment from the perspectives of communication and psycholinguistics.

Following these exploratory studies, we plan to measure *discriminate* alignment next. Here, priming spans across semantic relationships rather than only word identity (Swinney et al., 1979). Also, a next step would be to build a model that can quantify alignment (or even adaptation) and relate it to the factors pertinent to the discussion and the community, such as network measures and an individual propensity to align.

8 Acknowledgements

This research was made possible by a collaboration agreement between Penn State and the American Cancer Society. The authors would like to thank the society and collaborators Kenneth Portier and Greta E. Greer for their work in producing the CSN dataset, as well as Prasenjit Mitra and Yang Xu.

References

Lars Backstrom, Jon Kleinberg, Lillian Lee, and Cristian Danescu-Niculescu-Mizil. Characterizing and curating conversation threads: expansion, focus, volume, re-entry. In *Proceedings of the sixth ACM international conference on Web search and data mining*, pages 13–22. ACM, 2013.

Antonina Bambina. *Online social support: the interplay of social networks and computer-mediated communication.* Cambria press, 2007.

Christopher E Beaudoin and Chen-Chao Tao. Modeling the impact of online cancer resources on supporters of cancer patients. *New Media & Society*, 10(2):321–344, 2008.

J Kathryn Bock. Syntactic persistence in language production. *Cognitive psychology*, 18(3):355–387, 1986.

Kathryn Bock and Zenzi M Griffin. The persistence of structural priming: Transient activation or implicit learning? *Journal of Experimental Psychology: General*, 129(2):177, 2000.

Holly P. Branigan, Martin J. Pickering, and Alexandra A. Cleland. Syntactic priming in language production: Evidence for rapid decay. *Psychonomic Bulletin and Review*, 6(4):635–640, 1999.

Holly P Branigan, Martin J Pickering, and Alexandra A Cleland. Syntactic co-ordination in dialogue. *Cognition*, 75(2):B13–B25, 2000.

Holly P Branigan, Martin J Pickering, Jamie Pearson, and Janet F McLean. Linguistic alignment between people and computers. *Journal of Pragmatics*, 42(9):2355–2368, 2010.

Kenneth W. Church. Empirial estimates of adaptation: The chance of two Noriegas is closer to $p/2$ than p^2. In *Proceedings of the 18th Conference on Computational Linguistics (COLING)*, pages 180–186, Saarbrücken, Germany, 2000.

Cristian Danescu-Niculescu-Mizil and Lillian Lee. Chameleons in imagined conversations: A new approach to understanding coordination of linguistic style in dialogs. In *Proceedings of the 2nd Workshop on Cognitive Modeling and Computational Linguistics*, pages 76–87. Association for Computational Linguistics, 2011.

Cristian Danescu-Niculescu-Mizil, Michael Gamon, and Susan Dumais. Mark my words!: linguistic style accommodation in social media. In *Proceedings of the 20th international conference on World Wide Web*, pages 745–754. ACM, 2011.

Christine Dunkel-Schetter. Social support and cancer: Findings based on patient interviews and their implications. *Journal of Social Issues*, 40(4):77–98, 1984.

Victor Ferreira and Kathryn Bock. The functions of structural priming. *Language and Cognitive Processes*, 21(7-8): 1011–1029, 2006.

Riccardo Fusaroli, Bahador Bahrami, Karsten Olsen, Andreas Roepstorff, Geraint Rees, Chris Frith, and Kristian Tylén. Coming to terms quantifying the benefits of linguistic coordination. *Psychological Science*, 23(8): 931–939, 2012.

Simon Garrod and Martin J Pickering. Joint action, interactive alignment, and dialog. *Topics in Cognitive Science*, 1(2):292–304, 2009.

Stefan Th. Gries. Syntactic priming: A corpus-based approach. *Journal of Psycholinguistic Research*, 34(4): 365–399, 2005.

Patrick GT Healey and Gregory Mills. Participation, precedence and co-ordination in dialogue. In *Proceedings of the 28th Annual Conference of the Cognitive Science Society*, pages 1470–1475, 2006.

David Huffaker, Joseph Jorgensen, Francisco Iacobelli, Paul Tepper, and Justine Cassell. Computational measures for language similarity across time in online communities. In *Proceedings of the HLT-NAACL 2006 Workshop on Analyzing Conversations in Text and Speech*, pages 15–22. Association for Computational Linguistics, 2006.

T. Florian Jaeger and Neal Snider. Implicit learning and syntactic persistence: Surprisal and cumulativity. *University of Rochester Working Papers in the Language Sciences*, 3(1):26–44, 2007.

Michael P Kaschak, Timothy J Kutta, and John L Jones. Structural priming as implicit learning: Cumulative priming effects and individual differences. *Psychonomic Bulletin & Review*, 18(6):1133–1139, 2011a.

Michael P Kaschak, Timothy J Kutta, and Christopher Schatschneider. Long-term cumulative structural priming persists for (at least) one week. *Memory & Cognition*, 39 (3):381–388, 2011b.

Dan Klein and Christopher D Manning. Fast exact inference with a factored model for natural language parsing. *Advances in Neural Information Processing Systems*, pages 3–10, 2003.

Martin J Pickering and Victor S Ferreira. Structural priming: a critical review. *Psychological Bulletin*, 134(3):427, 2008.

Martin J Pickering and Simon Garrod. The interactive-alignment model: Developments and refinements. *Behavioral and Brain Sciences*, 27 (02):212–225, 2004.

Kenneth Portier, Greta E Greer, Lior Rokach, Nir Ofek, Yafei Wang, Prakhar Biyani, Mo Yu, Siddhartha Banerjee, Kang Zhao, Prasenjit Mitra, et al. Understanding topics and sentiment in an online cancer survivor community. *JNCI Monographs*, 2013(47):195–198, 2013.

Baojun Qiu, Kang Zhao, Prasenjit Mitra, Dinghao Wu, Cornelia Caragea, John Yen, Greta E Greer, and Kenneth Portier. Get online support, feel better–sentiment analysis and dynamics in an online cancer survivor community. In *Privacy, security, risk and trust (passat), 2011 ieee third international conference on and 2011 ieee third international conference on social computing (socialcom)*, pages 274–281. IEEE, 2011.

David Reitter and Johanna D Moore. Predicting success in dialogue. In *Annual Meeting of the Association for Computational Linguistics*, volume 45, page 808, 2007.

David Reitter, Johanna D. Moore, and Frank Keller. Priming of syntactic rules in task-oriented dialogue and spontaneous conversation. In *Proceedings of the 28th Annual Conference of the Cognitive Science Society (CogSci)*, pages 685–690, Vancouver, Canada, 2006.

David Reitter, Frank Keller, and Johanna D. Moore. A computational cognitive model of syntactic priming. *Cognitive Science*, 35(4):587–637, 2011.

Shelly Rodgers and Qimei Chen. Internet community group participation: Psychosocial benefits for women with breast cancer. *Journal of Computer-Mediated Communication*, 10(4):00–00, 2005.

Lauren E Scissors, Alastair J Gill, and Darren Gergle. Linguistic mimicry and trust in text-based cmc. In *Proceedings of the 2008 ACM Conference on Computer Supported Cooperative Work*, pages 277–280. ACM, 2008.

Svetlana Stenchikova and Amanda Stent. Measuring adaptation between dialogs. In *Proc. of the 8th SIGdial Workshop on Discourse and Dialogue*. Citeseer, 2007.

David Swinney, W. Onifer, P. Prather, and M. Hirshkowitz. Semantic facilitation across modalities in the processing of individual words and sentences. *Memory and Cognition*, 7:159–165, 1979.

Andrew J Winzelberg, Catherine Classen, Georg W Alpers, Heidi Roberts, Cheryl Koopman, Robert E Adams, Heidemarie Ernst, Parvati Dev, and C Barr Taylor. Evaluation of an internet support group for women with primary breast cancer. *Cancer*, 97(5):1164–1173, 2003.

Kang Zhao, John Yen, Greta Greer, Baojun Qiu, Prasenjit Mitra, and Kenneth Portier. Finding inuential users of online health communities: a new metric based on sentiment inuence. *J Am Med Inform Assoc*, 2014. doi: 10.1136/amiajnl-2013-002282.

Quantifying the role of discourse topicality in speakers' choices of referring expressions

Naho Orita
Department of Linguistics
University of Maryland
naho@umd.edu

Eliana Vornov
Departments of Computer Science and Linguistics
University of Maryland
evornov@umd.edu

Naomi H. Feldman
Department of Linguistics
University of Maryland
nhf@umd.edu

Jordan Boyd-Graber
College of Information Studies and UMIACS
University of Maryland
jbg@umiacs.umd.edu

Abstract

The salience of an entity in the discourse is correlated with the type of referring expression that speakers use to refer to that entity. Speakers tend to use pronouns to refer to salient entities, whereas they use lexical noun phrases to refer to less salient entities. We propose a novel approach to formalize the interaction between salience and choices of referring expressions using topic modeling, focusing specifically on the notion of topicality. We show that topic models can capture the observation that topical referents are more likely to be pronominalized. This lends support to theories of discourse salience that appeal to latent topic representations and suggests that topic models can capture aspects of speakers' cognitive representations of entities in the discourse.

1 Introduction

Speakers' choices of referring expressions (pronouns, demonstratives, full names, and so on) have been used as a tool to understand cognitive representations of entities in a discourse. Many researchers have proposed a correlation between the type of a referring form and *saliency* (or *accessibility*, *prominence*, *focus*) of the entity in the discourse (Chafe, 1976; Gundel et al., 1993; Brennan, 1995; Ariel, 1990). Because a pronoun carries less information compared to more specified forms (e.g., *she* vs. *Hillary Clinton*), theories predict that speakers tend to use pronouns when they think that a referent is sufficiently salient in the discourse. When the referent is less salient, more specified forms are used. In other words, the likelihood of pronominalization increases as referents become more salient.

Topic modeling (Blei et al., 2003; Griffiths et al., 2007) uses a probabilistic model that recovers a latent topic representation from observed words in a document. The model assumes that words appearing in documents have been generated from a mixture of latent topics. These latent topics have been argued to provide a coarse semantic representation of documents and to be in close correspondence with many aspects of human semantic cognition (Griffiths et al., 2007). This previous work has focused on semantic relationships among words and documents. While it is often assumed that the topics extracted by topic models correspond to the gist of a document, and although topic models have been used to capture discourse-level properties in some settings (Nguyen et al., 2013), the ability of topic models to capture cognitive aspects of speakers' discourse representations has not yet been tested.

In this paper we use topic modeling to formalize the idea of salience in the discourse. We focus specifically on the idea of topicality as a predictor of salience (Ariel, 1990; Arnold, 1998) and ask whether the latent topics that are recovered by topic models can predict speakers' choices of referring expressions. Simulations show that the referents of pronouns belong, on average, to higher probability topics than the referents of full noun phrases, indicating that topical referents are more likely to be pronominalized. This suggests that

Proceedings of the 2014 ACL Workshop on Cognitive Modeling and Computational Linguistics, pages 63–70,
Baltimore, Maryland USA, June 26 2014. ©2014 Association for Computational Linguistics

the information recovered by topic models is relevant to speakers' choices of referring expressions and that topic models can provide a useful tool for quantifying speakers' representations of entities in the discourse.

The structure of this paper is as follows. Section 2 briefly reviews studies that look at the correlation between saliency and choices of referring expression, focusing on topicality, and introduces our approach to this problem. Section 3 describes a model that learns a latent topic distribution and formalizes the notion of topicality within this framework. Section 4 describes the data we used for our simulation. Section 5 shows simulation results. Section 6 discusses implications and future directions.

2 Saliency and referring expressions

Various factors have been proposed to influence referent salience (Arnold, 1998; Arnold, 2010). These factors include **giveness** (Chafe, 1976; Gundel et al., 1993), **grammatical position** (Brennan, 1995; Stevenson et al., 1994), **order of mention** (Järvikivi et al., 2005; Kaiser and Trueswell, 2008), **recency** (Givón, 1983; Arnold, 1998), **syntactic focus and syntactic topic** (Cowles et al., 2007; Foraker and McElree, 2007; Walker et al., 1994), **parallelism** (Chambers and Smyth, 1998; Arnold, 1998), **thematic role** (Stevenson et al., 1994; Arnold, 2001; Rohde et al., 2007), **coherence relation** (Kehler, 2002; Rohde et al., 2007) and **topicality** (Ariel, 1990; Arnold, 1998; Arnold, 1999). Psycholinguistic experiments (Arnold, 1998; Arnold, 2001; Kaiser, 2006) show that determining the salient referent is a complex process which is affected by various sources of information, and that these multiple factors have different strengths of influence.

Among the numerous factors influencing the salience of a referent, this study focuses on *topicality*. In contrast to surface-level factors such as grammatical position, order of mention, and recency, the representation of topicality is latent and requires inference. Because of this latent representation, it has been challenging to investigate the role of topicality in discourse.

Many researchers have observed that there is a correlation between a linguistic category "topic" and referent salience and have suggested that topical referents are more likely to be pronominalized (Ariel, 1990; Dahl and Fraurud, 1996). However, Arnold (2010) points out that examining the relation between topicality and choices of referring expressions is difficult for two reasons. First, identifying the topic is known to be hard. Arnold (2010) shows that it is hard to determine what the topic is even in a simple sentence like *Andy brews beer* (Is the topic *Andy*, *beer*, or *brewing*?). Second, researchers have defined the notion of "topic" differently as follows.

- The topic is often defined as what the sentence is about (Reinhart, 1981).
- The topic can be defined as prominent characters such as the protagonist (Francik, 1985).
- The topic is often associated with old information (Gundel et al., 1993).
- The subject position is considered to be a topical position (Chafe, 1976).
- Repeated mentions are topical (Kameyama, 1994).
- Psycholinguistic experiments define a discourse topic as a referent that has already been mentioned in the preceding discourse as a pronoun/the topic of a cleft (Arnold, 1999) or realized in subject position (Cowles, 2003).
- Centering theory (Grosz et al., 1995; Brennan, 1995) formalizes the topic as a backward-looking center that is a single entity mentioned in the last sentence and in the most salient grammatical position (the grammatical subject is the most salient, and followed by the object and oblique object).
- Givón (1983) suggests that all discourse entities are topical but that topicality is defined by a gradient/continuous property. Givón shows that three measures of topicality – *recency* (the distance between the referent and the referring expression), *persistence* (how long the referent would remain in the subsequent discourse), and *potential interference* (how many other potential referents of the referring expression there are in the preceding discourse) – correlate with the types of reference expressions. Note that these scales measure topicality of the *referring expression*, but not the referent per se.

The variation in the literature seems to derive from three fundamental properties. First, as Arnold (2010) pointed out, there is variation in the linguistic unit that bears the topic. For example, Reinhart (1981) defines each *sentence* as having a single topic, whereas Givón (1983) defines each *entity* as having a single topic. Second, there is a variation in type of variable. For example, Givón (1983) defines topicality as a continuous property, whereas Centering seems to treat topicality as categorical based on the grammatical position of the referent. Third, many studies define 'topic' as a combination of surface linguistic factors such as grammatical position and recency. When topicality is defined in terms of meaning, as in Reinhart (1981), we face difficulty in identifying *what the topic is*, as summarized in Arnold (1998). None of the existing definitions/measures seem to provide a way to capture latent topic representations, and this makes it challenging to investigate their role in discourse representations. It is this idea of latent topic representations that we aim to formalize.

Our study investigates whether topic modeling (Blei et al., 2003; Griffiths et al., 2007) can be used to formalize the relationship between topicality and choices of referring expressions. Because of their structured representations, consisting of a set of topics as well as information about which words belong to those topics, topic models are able to capture topicality by means of semantic associations. For example, observing a word *Clinton* increases the topicality of other words associated with the topic that *Clinton* belongs to, e.g., *president*, *Washington* and so on. In other words, topic models can capture not only the salience of referents within a document, but also the salience of referents via the structured topic representation learned from multiple texts.

We use topic modeling to verify the prevailing hypothesis that topical referents are more likely to be pronominalized than lexical nouns. Examining the relationship between topicality and referring expressions using topic modeling provides an opportunity to test how well the representation recovered by topic models corresponds to the cognitive representation of entities in a discourse. If we can recover the observation that topical referents are more likely to be pronominalized than more specified forms, this could indicate that topic models can capture not only aspects of human semantic cognition (Griffiths et al., 2007), but also aspects of a higher level of linguistic representation, discourse.

3 Model

3.1 Recovering latent topics

We formalize topicality of referents using topic modeling. Each document is represented as a probability distribution over topics. Each topic is represented as a probability distribution over possible referents in the corpus. In training our topic model, we assume that all lexical nouns in the discourse are potential referents. The topic model is trained only on lexical nouns, excluding all other words. This ensures that the latent topics capture information about which referents typically occur together in documents.[1]

Rather than pre-specifying a number of latent topics, we use the hierarchical Dirichlet process (Teh et al., 2006), which learns a number of topics to flexibly represent input data. The summary of the generative process is as follows.

1. Draw a global topic distribution $G_0 \sim \text{DP}(\gamma, H)$ (where γ is a hyperparameter and H is a base distribution).
2. For each document $d \in \{1, \ldots, D\}$ (where D denotes the number of documents in the corpus),
   (a) draw a document-topic distribution $G_d \sim \text{DP}(\alpha_0, G_0)$ (where α_0 is a hyperparameter).
   (b) For each referent $r \in \{1, \ldots, N_d\}$ (where N_d denotes the number of referents in document d),
      i. draw a topic parameter $\phi_{d,r} \sim G_d$.
      ii. draw a word $x_{d,r} \sim \text{Mult}(\phi_{d,r})$.

This process generates a distribution over topics for each document, a distribution over referents for each topic, and a topic assignment for each referent. The distribution over topics for each document represents what the topics of the document are. The distribution over referents for each topic represents what the topic is about. An illustration of this representation is in Table 3.1. Topics and words that appear in the second and third columns are ordered from highest to lowest. We can represent topicality of the referents using this

[1]Excluding pronouns from the training set introduces a confound, because it artificially lowers the probability of the topics corresponding to those pronouns. However, in this paper our predicted effect goes in the opposite direction: we predict that topics corresponding to the referents of pronouns will have higher probability than those corresponding to the referents of lexical nouns. Excluding pronouns thus makes us less likely to find support for our hypothesis.

probabilistic latent topic representation, measuring which topics have high probability and assuming that referents associated with high probability topics are likely to be topical in the discourse.

Word	Top 3 topic IDs	Associated words in the 1st topic
Clinton	5, 26, 61	president, meeting, peace, Washington, talks
FBI	148, 73, 67	Leung, charges, Katrina, documents, indictment
oil	91, 145, 140	Burmah, Iraq, SHV, coda, pipeline

Table 1: Illustration of the topic distribution

Given this generative process, we can use Bayesian inference to recover the latent topic distribution. We use the Gibbs sampling algorithm in Teh et al. (2006) to estimate the conditional distribution of the latent structure, the distributions over topics associated with each document, and the distributions over words associated with each topic. The state space consists of latent variables for topic assignments, which we refer to as $\mathbf{z} = \{z_{d,r}\}$. In each iteration we compute the conditional distribution $p(z_{d,r}|\mathbf{x}, \mathbf{z}_{-d,r}, *)$, where the subscript $-d, r$ denotes counts without considering $z_{d,r}$ and $*$ denotes all hyperparameters. Recovering these latent variables allows us to determine what the topic of the referent is and how likely that topic is in a particular document. We use the latent topic and its probability to represent topicality.

3.2 A measure of topicality

Discourse theories predict that topical referents are more likely to be pronominalized than more specified expressions.[2] We can quantify the effect of topicality on choices of referring expressions by comparing the topicality of the referents of two types of referring expressions, pronouns and lexical nouns. If topical words are more likely to be pronominalized, then the topicality of the referents of pronouns should be higher than the topicality of the referents of lexical nouns.

Annotated coreference chains in the corpus, described below, are used to determine the referent of each referring expression. We look at the topic assigned to each referent r in document d by the topic model, $z_{d,r}$. We take the log probability of this topic within the document, $\log p(z_{d,r}|G_d)$, as a measure of the topicality of the referent. We take the expectation over a uniform distribution of referents, where the uniform distributions are denoted $u(lex)$ and $u(pro)$, to obtain an estimate of the average topicality of the referents of lexical nouns, $\mathbb{E}_{u(lex)}[\log p(z_{d,r}|G_d)]$, and the average topicality of the referents of pronouns, $\mathbb{E}_{u(pro)}[\log p(z_{d,r}|G_d)]$, within each document. The expectation for the referents of the pronouns in a document is computed as

$$\mathbb{E}_{u(pro)}[\log p(z_{d,r}|G_d)] = \frac{\sum_{r=1}^{N_{d,pro}} \log p(z_{d,r}|G_d)}{N_{d,pro}} \quad (1)$$

where $N_{d,pro}$ denotes the number of pronouns in a document d. Replacing $N_{d,pro}$ with $N_{d,lex}$ (the number of lexical nouns in a document d) gives us the expectation for the referents of lexical nouns.

To obtain a single measure for each document of the extent to which our measure of topicality predicts speakers' choices of referring expressions, we subtract the average topicality for the referents of lexical nouns from the average topicality for the referents of pronouns within the document to obtain a log likelihood ratio q_d,

$$q_d = \mathbb{E}_{u(pro)}[\log p(z_{d,r}|G_d)] - \mathbb{E}_{u(lex)}[\log p(z_{d,r}|G_d)] \quad (2)$$

A value of q_d greater than zero indicates that the referents of pronouns are more likely to be topical than the referents of lexical nouns.

4 Annotated coreference data

Our simulations use a training set of the Ontonotes corpus (Pradhan et al., 2007), which consists of news texts. We use these data because each entity in the corpus has a coreference annotation. We use the coreference annotations in our evaluation, described above. The training set in the corpus consists of 229 documents, which contain 3,648 sentences and 79,060 word tokens. We extract only lexical nouns (23,084 tokens) and pronouns (2,867 tokens) from the corpus as input to the model.[3]

Some preprocessing is necessary before using these data as input to a topic model. This necessity arises because some entities in the corpus are represented as phrases, such as in (1a) and (1b) below,

[2] Although theories make more fine-grained predictions on the choices of referring expressions with respect to saliency, e.g., a full name is used to refer to less salient entity compared to a definite description (c.f. accessibility marking scale in Ariel 1990), we focus here on the coarse contrast between pronouns and lexical nouns.

[3] In particular, we extracted words that are tagged as NN, NNS, NNP, NNPS, and for pronouns as PRP, PRP$.

where numbers following each expression represent the entity ID that is assigned to this expression in the annotated corpus. However, topic models use bag-of-words representations and therefore assign latent topic structure only to individual words, and not to entire phrases. We preprocessed these entities as in (2). This enabled us to attribute entity IDs to individual words, rather than entire phrases, allowing us to establish a correspondence between these ID numbers and the latent topics recovered by our model for the same words.

1. Before preprocessing
   (a) a tradition in Betsy's family: 352
   (b) Betsy's family: 348
   (c) Betsy: 184
2. After preprocessing
   (a) tradition: 352
   (b) family: 348
   (c) Betsy: 184

Annotated coreference chains in the corpus were used to determine the referent of each pronoun and lexical noun. The annotations group all referring expressions in a document that refer to the same entity together into one coreference chain, with the order of expressions in the chain corresponding to the order in which they appear in the document. We assume that the referent for each pronoun and lexical noun appears in its coreference chain. We further assume that the referent needs to be a lexical noun, and thus exclude all pronouns from consideration as referents. If a lexical noun does not have any other words before it in the coreference chain, i.e., that noun is the first or the only word in that coreference chain, we assume that this noun refers to itself (the noun itself is the referent). Otherwise, if a coreference chain has multiple referents, we take its referent to be the lexical noun that is before and closest to the target word.

5 Results

To recover the latent topic distribution, we ran 5 independent Gibbs sampling chains for 1000 iterations.[4] Hyperparameters γ, α_0, and η were fixed at 1.0, 1.0, and 0.01, respectively.[5] The model recovered an average of 161 topics (range: $160-163$ topics).

We computed the log likelihood ratio q_d (Equation 2) for each document and took the average of this value across documents for each chain. The formula to compute this average is as follows.

For each chain g,
1. get the final sample s in g.
2. For each document d in the corpus,
   i. compute q_d based on s.
3. Compute the average of all q_d in the corpus.

The average log likelihood ratio in each chain consistently shows values greater than zero across the 5 chains. The average log likelihood ratio across chains is 1.0625 with standard deviation 0.7329. As an example, in one chain, the average of the expected values for the referents of pronouns across documents is -1.1849 with standard deviation 0.8796. In the same chain, the average of the expected values for the referents of lexical nouns across documents is -2.2356 with standard deviation 0.5009.

We used the median test[6] to evaluate whether the two groups of the referents are different with respect to the expected values of the log probabilities of topics. The test shows a significant difference between two groups ($p < 0.0001$).

We also computed the probability density $p(q)$ from the log likelihood ratio q_d for each document using the final samples from each chain. Graph 1 shows the probability density $p(q)$ from each chain. The peak after zero confirms the observed effect.

Table 2 shows examples of target pronouns and lexical nouns, their referents, and the topic assigned to each referent from a document. Table 3 shows the distribution over topics in the document obtained from one chain. Topics in Table 3 are ordered from highest to lowest. Only four topics were present in this document. The list of referents associated with each topic in Table 3 is recovered from the topic distribution over referents. This list shows what the topic is about.

4 We used a Python version of the hierarchical Dirichlet process implemented by Ke Zhai (http://github.com/kzhai/PyNPB/tree/master/src/hdp).

5 Parameter γ controls how likely a new topic is to be created in the corpus. If the value of γ is high, more topics are discovered in the corpus. Parameter α_0 controls the sparseness of the distribution over topics in a document, and parameter η controls the sparseness of the distribution over words in a topic.

6 The median test compares medians to test group differences (Siegel, 1956).

Topic ID	Assciated words	Probability
1	Milosevic, Kostunica, Slobodan, president, Belgrade, Serbia, Vojislav, Yugoslavia, crimes, parliament	0.64
2	president, Clinton, meeting, peace, Washington, talks, visit, negotiators, region, ..., Alabanians	0.16
3	people, years, U.S., president, time, government, today, country, world, way, year	0.16
4	government, minister, party, Barak, today, prime, east, parliament, leader, opposition, peace, leadership	0.04

Table 3: The document-topic distribution

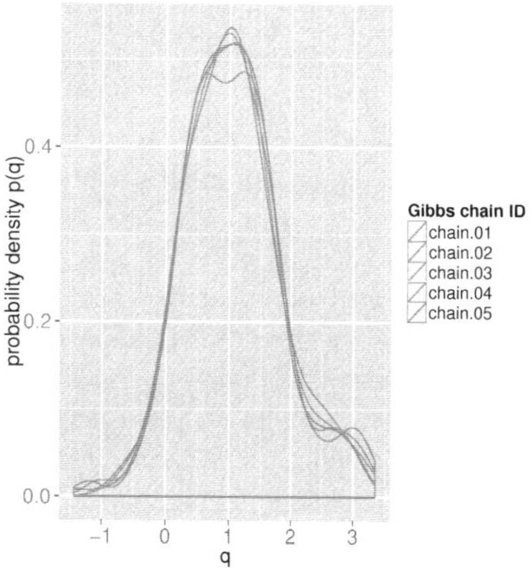

Figure 1: The probability density of $p(q)$

Target	Referent	Referent's Topic ID
his	Spilanovic	1
he	Spilanovic	1
its	Belgrade	1
Goran	Minister	4
Albanians	Albanians	2
Kosovo	Kosovo	1

Table 2: Target words, their corresponding referents, and the assigned topics of the referents

The topics associated with the pronouns *his*, *he* and *its* have the highest probability in the document-topic distribution, as shown in Table 3. In contrast, although the topic associated with the word *Kosovo* has the highest probability in the document-topic distribution, the topics associated with nouns *Goran* and *Albanians* do not have high probability in the document-topic distribution. This is an example from one document, but this tendency is observed in most of the documents in the corpus.

These results indicate that the referents of pronouns are more topical than the referents of lexical nouns using our measure of topicality derived from the topic model. This suggests that our measure of topicality captures aspects of salience that influence choices of referring expressions.

However, there is a possibility that the effect we observed is simply derived from referent frequencies and that topic modeling structure does not play a role beyond this. Tily and Piantadosi (2009) found that the frequency of referents has a significant effect on predicting the upcoming referent. Although their finding is about comprehender's ability to predict the upcoming referent (not the type of referring expression), we conducted an additional analysis to rule out the possibility that referent frequencies alone were driving our results.

In order to quantify the effect of referent frequency on choices of referring expressions, we computed the same log likelihood ratio q_d with referent probabilities. The probability of a referent in a document was computed as follows:

$$p(r_i|doc_d) = \frac{C_{d,r_i}}{C_{d,\cdot}} \qquad (3)$$

where C_{d,r_i} denotes the number of mentions that refer to referent r_i in document d and $C_{d,\cdot}$ denotes the total number of mentions in document d. We can directly compute this value by using the annotated coreference chains in the corpus.

The log likelihood ratio for this measure is 2.3562. The average of the expected values for the referents of pronouns across documents is -1.1993 with standard deviation 0.6812. The average of the expected values for the referents of lexical nouns across documents is -3.5556 with standard deviation 0.9742. The median test shows a significant difference between two groups. ($p < 0.0001$). These results indicate that the frequency of a referent captures aspects of its salience that influence choices of referring expressions, raising the question of whether our latent topic representations capture something that simple referent frequencies do not.

In order to examine to what extent the relationship between topicality and referring expressions captures information that goes beyond simple referent frequencies, we compare two logistic regression models.[7] Both models are built to predict whether a referent will be a full noun phrase or a pronoun. The first model incorporates only the log probability of the referent as a predictor, whereas the second includes both the log probability of the referent and our topicality measure as predictors.[8]

The null hypothesis is that removing our topicality measure from the second model makes no difference for predicting the types of referring expressions. Under this null hypothesis, twice the difference in the log likelihoods between the two models should follow a $\chi^2(1)$ distribution. We find a significant difference in likelihood between these two models ($\chi^2(1) = 118.38, p < 0.0001$), indicating that the latent measure of topicality derived from the topic model predicts aspects of listeners' choices of referring expressions that are not predicted by the probabilities of individual referents.

6 Discussion

In this study we formalized the correlation between topicality and choices of referring expressions using a latent topic representation obtained through topic modeling. Both quantitative and qualitative results showed that according to this latent topic representation, the referents of pronouns are more likely to be topical than the referents of lexical nouns. This suggests that topic models can capture aspects of discourse representations that are relevant to the selection of referring expressions. We also showed that this latent topic representation has an independent contribution beyond simple referent frequency.

This study examined only two independent factors: topicality and referent frequency. However, discourse studies suggest that the salience of a referent is determined by various sources of information and multiple discourse factors with different strengths of influence (Arnold, 2010). Our framework could eventually form part of a more complex model that explicitly formalizes the interaction of information source and various discourse factors. Having a formal model would help by allowing us to test different hypotheses and develop a firm theory regarding cognitive representations of entities in the discourse.

One possibility for exploring the role of various discourse factors in our framework is to use recent advances in topic modeling. For example, TagLDA (Zhu et al., 2006) includes part-of-speech as part of the model, and syntactic topic models (Boyd-Graber and Blei, 2008) incorporate syntactic information. Whereas simulations in our study only used nouns as input, it has been observed that the thematic role of the entity influences referent salience (Stevenson et al., 1994; Arnold, 2001; Rohde et al., 2007). Using part-of-speech and syntactic information together with the topic information could help us approximate the influence of the thematic role and allow us to simulate how this factor interacts with latent topic information and other factors.

It has been challenging to quantify the influence of latent factors such as topicality, and the simulations in this paper represent only a first step toward capturing these challenging factors. The simulations nevertheless provide an example of how formal models can help us validate theories of the relationship between speakers' discourse representations and the language they produce.

Acknowledgments

We thank Ke Zhai, Viet-An Nguyen, and four anonymous reviewers for helpful comments and discussion.

References

Mira Ariel. 1990. *Accessing noun-phrase antecedents*. Routledge, London.

Jennifer Arnold. 1998. *Reference form and discourse patterns*. Ph.D. thesis, Stanford University Stanford, CA.

Jennifer Arnold. 1999. Marking salience: The similarity of topic and focus. *Unpublished manuscript, University of Pennsylvania.*

Jennifer Arnold. 2001. The effect of thematic roles on pronoun use and frequency of reference continuation. *Discourse Processes*, 31(2):137–162.

Jennifer Arnold. 2010. How speakers refer: the role of accessibility. *Language and Linguistics Compass*, 4(4):187–203.

David M Blei, Andrew Y Ng, and Michael I Jordan. 2003. Latent Dirichlet allocation. *Journal of Machine Learning Research*, 3:993–1022.

Jordan L Boyd-Graber and David M Blei. 2008. Syntactic topic models. In *Neural Information Processing Systems*, pages 185–192.

[7] Models were fit using `glm` in R. For the log-likelihood ratio test, `lrtest` in R package `epicalc` was used.

[8] We also ran a version of this comparison in which frequency of mention was included as a predictor in both models, and obtained similar results.

Susan E Brennan. 1995. Centering attention in discourse. *Language and Cognitive Processes*, 10(2):137–167.

Wallace Chafe. 1976. Givenness, contrastiveness, definiteness, subjects, topics, and point of view. In C. N. Li, editor, *Subject and Topic*. Academic Press, New York.

Craig G Chambers and Ron Smyth. 1998. Structural parallelism and discourse coherence: A test of Centering theory. *Journal of Memory and Language*, 39(4):593–608.

H Wind Cowles, Matthew Walenski, and Robert Kluender. 2007. Linguistic and cognitive prominence in anaphor resolution: topic, contrastive focus and pronouns. *Topoi*, 26(1):3–18.

Heidi Wind Cowles. 2003. *Processing information structure: Evidence from comprehension and production*. Ph.D. thesis, University of California, San Diego.

Osten Dahl and Kari Fraurud. 1996. Animacy in grammar and discourse. *Pragmatics and Beyond New Series*, pages 47–64.

Stephani Foraker and Brian McElree. 2007. The role of prominence in pronoun resolution: Active versus passive representations. *Journal of Memory and Language*, 56(3):357–383.

Ellen Palmer Francik. 1985. *Referential choice and focus of attention in narratives (discourse anaphora, topic continuity, language production)*. Ph.D. thesis, Stanford University.

Talmy Givón. 1983. *Topic continuity in discourse: A quantitative cross-language study*, volume 3. John Benjamins Publishing.

Thomas L Griffiths, Mark Steyvers, and Joshua B Tenenbaum. 2007. Topics in semantic representation. *Psychological Review*, 114(2):211.

Barbara J Grosz, Scott Weinstein, and Aravind K Joshi. 1995. Centering: A framework for modeling the local coherence of discourse. *Computational Linguistics*, 21(2):203–225.

Jeanette K Gundel, Nancy Hedberg, and Ron Zacharski. 1993. Cognitive status and the form of referring expressions in discourse. *Language*, pages 274–307.

Juhani Järvikivi, Roger PG van Gompel, Jukka Hyönä, and Raymond Bertram. 2005. Ambiguous pronoun resolution contrasting the first-mention and subject-preference accounts. *Psychological Science*, 16(4):260–264.

Elsi Kaiser and John C Trueswell. 2008. Interpreting pronouns and demonstratives in Finnish: Evidence for a form-specific approach to reference resolution. *Language and Cognitive Processes*, 23(5):709–748.

Elsi Kaiser. 2006. Effects of topic and focus on salience. In *Proceedings of Sinn und Bedeutung*, volume 10, pages 139–154. Citeseer.

Megumi Kameyama. 1994. Indefeasible semantics and defeasible pragmatics. In *CWI Report CS-R9441 and SRI Technical Note 544*. Citeseer.

Andrew Kehler. 2002. *Coherence, reference, and the theory of grammar*. CSLI publications, Stanford, CA.

Viet-An Nguyen, Jordan Boyd-Graber, Philip Resnik, Deborah A Cai, Jennifer E Midberry, and Yuanxin Wang. 2013. Modeling topic control to detect influence in conversations using nonparametric topic models. *Machine Learning*, pages 1–41.

Sameer S Pradhan, Eduard Hovy, Mitch Marcus, Martha Palmer, Lance Ramshaw, and Ralph Weischedel. 2007. Ontonotes: A unified relational semantic representation. *International Journal of Semantic Computing*, 1(4):405–419.

Tanya Reinhart. 1981. Pragmatics and linguistics: An analysis of sentence topics in pragmatics and philosophy I. *Philosophica*, 27(1):53–94.

Hannah Rohde, Andrew Kehler, and Jeffrey L Elman. 2007. Pronoun interpretation as a side effect of discourse coherence. In *Proceedings of the 29th Annual Conference of the Cognitive Science Society*, pages 617–622.

Sidney Siegel. 1956. *Nonparametric statistics for the behavioral sciences*. McGraw-Hill.

Rosemary J Stevenson, Rosalind A Crawley, and David Kleinman. 1994. Thematic roles, focus and the representation of events. *Language and Cognitive Processes*, 9(4):519–548.

Y. W. Teh, M. I. Jordan, M. J. Beal, and D. M. Blei. 2006. Hierarchical Dirichlet processes. *Journal of the American Statistical Association*, 101:1566–1581.

Harry Tily and Steven Piantadosi. 2009. Refer efficiently: Use less informative expressions for more predictable meanings. In *Proceedings of the workshop on the production of referring expressions: Bridging the gap between computational and empirical approaches to reference*.

Marilyn Walker, Sharon Cote, and Masayo Iida. 1994. Japanese discourse and the process of centering. *Computational Linguistics*, 20(2):193–232.

Xiaojin Zhu, David Blei, and John Lafferty. 2006. TagLDA: Bringing document structure knowledge into topic models. Technical report, Technical Report TR-1553, University of Wisconsin.

Author Index